Chakras for Beginners

Table of Contents

Introduction
Chapter One: The Energy Body
Chapter Two: Chakras and Colors
Chapter Three: The Root Chakra - Muladhara
Chapter Four: The Sacral Chakra - Svadisthana
Chapter Five: The Solar Plexus Chakra - Manipura
Chapter Six: The Heart Chakra - Anahata
Chapter Seven: The Throat Chakra - Vishuddha
Chapter Eight: The Third Eye Chakra - Ajna
Chapter Nine: The Crown Chakra - Sahasrara
Chapter Ten: Meditation and Breathing Exercises
Chapter Eleven: Positive Affirmations
Chapter Twelve: Developing Your Psychic Abilities
Conclusion
Here's another book by Mari Silva that you might like
References

Introduction

You're about to begin a journey that is magical. One that will completely change your life and make you see beyond the veil that keeps your spirit shrouded from the material world. You're about to explore other aspects of yourself that, up until this point, you may not have known existed. You're about to uncover the wonderful world of chakras and how they can help you live a fuller, richer, more rewarding life on all levels of existence.

For the most part, when problems come up in our day-to-day lives, affecting our health, wealth, relationships, or careers, we turn to every external solution we can to fix them. Do you have a bothersome, recurring migraine? Pop an Advil. Can't stay awake at work? Chug two more espressos. Not enough money, no matter what you do? Ask for a raise or take on an extra job. Sure, these are practical solutions, but the physical world is that all problems have an energetic source. It is best to address these problems not just with physical action but on an energetic level. This is where your chakras come into play.

You will learn about how these energy centers affect your life and what you can do to keep them balanced, clear, active, and in alignment. Most people have chakras that haven't been active in ages, and because of this, they suffer the consequences. Have you ever met someone who's always afraid of everything? What about someone who's very distrusting? Or someone who, no matter what they do and how many ventures they get into, they just never make enough money? What about those who make a killing but never seem able to hold on to it?

Well, you're about to discover how the chakras play a role in those personality traits and how spending a few minutes every day to give them a tune-up can revolutionize every aspect of your life. So many people go through their lives facing needless challenges and issues that could be resolved if only they knew about the chakra system and how it affects everything they do. Sadly, people are quick to dismiss concepts about chakras as hogwash without bothering to learn more. You're here, though, which means you know better.

As you read this, I invite you to set aside your preconceived notions of what science says is true and isn't true. Just because something, as of now, cannot be perceived with the physical senses or measured with tools doesn't mean it doesn't exist. That you're reading this right now makes it clear you're aware that there's more to life than meets the senses. So, keep that energy up as you read through, and commit to yourself right here and now that you will practice what you learn and prove it to yourself. After all, there's no better proof than your own experience, especially in matters of spirituality.

Chapter One: The Energy Body

Your physical body isn't the only one you have. You have an energy body as well, that is like a subtle framework for your physical body. You will find there are many approaches to working with your energy body. However, the goal remains to stimulate this part of you and to develop yourself spiritually so your entire life is one full of health, purpose, and joy.

Just because you can't see your energy body doesn't mean it has no importance. It is essential for total health and wellness. You may have heard terms like Prana, Chi, Orgone, Huna, Odic Force, Life Force, and so on. These are various ways life energy is described. Yoga, Qi Gung, Reiki, Tai Chi, Pranic Healing, Reflexology, Quantum Touch, Acupuncture, Kung Fu, are all founded on the principle of energy.

More Energy, More Life

To put this simply, the more you take care of your energy body, the more energy you have in every aspect of your life, in terms of your physical wellbeing, emotions, creativity, and spirituality. Working with your energy body is also a sure-fire way to grow and develop your psychic abilities since energy is needed to sense things that lie outside the typical range of human perception, often limited to the five senses.

Everything that happens in your body, such as the healing of flesh and bone, the beating of your heart, brain function, digestion, and emotions, is based on energy. All this swirling activity comes together to form an electromagnetic field that emanates from you. Your heart is the one organ that produces this field the most, considering this energy can stretch as far as 15 feet from you. According to Oschman and Pert in *Energy Medicine*, this energy has been measured with people who are natural healers or who work with energy, and the field they generate is significant.

Subtle Energy and Your Energy Body

There are many ways this subtle energy moves through your energy body. Besides the food you eat and the stuff you drink, your energy body receives subtle energy from the Earth itself and the air. You will find this same subtle energy coming from the Sun, the same self-energy that keeps everything in the universe running and staying on course.

You exchange energy with all people and things around you. Consider this: Everything that is matter is energy. The entire world and your very self — the macrocosm and microcosm — are all energy, expressed in various ways. This includes non-living things. We're all intricately connected on an energy level.

What the Energy Body Is

As you are right now, all your body's cells are highly active and full of bioelectricity, which generates your biomagnetic fields. Beyond all the cellular activity lies your subtle energy field and your spiritual energy field. These two fields are what make up your energy body. Though subtle, this body is just as complex and intricate as your physical one, even though it's not immediately easy to detect the structures that it has. Truth be told, there is only one tool that can detect the subtle body: humans. The ability to detect this requires sensitivity to energy.

For you to understand your energy body, you need to learn how to feel the energy in you and work with it. You're going to learn how to do this in this book so that you know without a shadow of a doubt that you do have a subtle double that you can work with.

While the energy body serves as a framework for the physical body, the fact is there are certain areas and conditions in which it functions all by itself. For instance, people who have lost a limb will often talk about feeling a shadow version of it there, and they're not just missing that limb or imagining it. They're sensing the energy body, which is still whole and continues to do its thing. In fact, Kirlian photography reveals that the energy version of that limb is still very present and active.

Layers of Energy

There are various layers to your subtle body. It has several energy centers, or chakras if you prefer that term. These centers are essentially the equivalent of a vital organ in your physical body. Let's look at what's going on with this body. Here are the parts you need to be most aware of:

- The primary energy centers comprise the seven major chakras.
- The secondary centers, numbering in the hundreds
- The three storage centers
- Tertiary centers, which are tiny pores through which energy is exchanged
- The Sushumna or central channel, which is a central channel that runs through the middle of the body
- Two conduits for the energy that goes through Sushumna: Ida and Pingala

    The Ida and Pingala both wind up either side of the Sushumna. The perfect visual representation is the symbol for the staff of Hermes, also called the Caduceus.

    For working with the energy body, you want to think about it as simply as you can, focusing on the basic structures that exist. We'll focus on the chakras, energy storage centers, and exchange pores only.

Energy Work

Your thoughts and feelings affect the energy body. When you're in a great mood, it will naturally grow, expand, and give you more life and power. When you feel awful, it will shrink, draining you of all your zest for life. Doing energy work is a great way to make sure that your body and mind are in great health at every level. The more you're aware of your body, the more energy flows. As the saying goes, "Energy flows where attention goes." When you work on growing more and more aware of your body, you will experience growth and a connection to much higher levels of spirituality.

Traditional energy work involves moving the physical body, visualization, stretching, breathing, chanting, holding specific postures, and toning — these work to improve the flow of life force through your subtle energy body in many ways. The New Age methods are more about you using relaxation techniques along with visualization. Visualization is a bit of a problem because most people don't understand what it is and think they can't do it.

Tactile Imaging

The exercises that you'll learn here are based on the tactile imaging system developed by Robert Bruce, which, fortunately, needs no visualization on your part. He developed this system when a couple of people – blind from birth –contacted him for assistance with their energy work, seeing as they couldn't "visualize." According to Bruce, he figured that while they might not have been able to work with sight, the rest of their senses would be even more heightened than the average person's. His experiments led to him discovering this brilliant method, which you will learn shortly.

With tactile imaging, you have only to put all your attention on a particular part or spot on your body. Doing this will cause your energy body to receive stimulation. It's the most effective and the simplest method you could use, and so you'd be better off sticking with this one.

The Importance of Energy Work

For most people, their energy bodies' structures are dormant, working only just enough to allow their physical body to do the necessary things and nothing more. It doesn't work enough to allow any spiritual growth or development. There are two ways they stop being dormant: spontaneously or through actual energy work and spiritual practice. The obvious question is: Since the energy body is doing the bare minimum needed to sustain the physical, why bother with trying to wake it up?

There are so many benefits to be experienced from becoming aware of this subtle body and deliberately working with it. It will grant your visible body levels of strength and health simply amazing. You'll heal faster, and you'll be much better at resisting diseases. With enough practice, you can also activate the self-healing systems in your body to work exactly as you need them to with injuries and illnesses that affect specific body parts.

There are several parallels you can draw between the physical body and the energy one. Energy or life force is as important as the blood in your veins. Workout, eat right, stay hydrated, sleep well, and your physical body will get stronger and healthier. In the same way, your energy body can grow in vitality when you do the right things to help it grow.

To work with your chakras and develop them fully, then you cannot escape energy work. The curious thing is that everyone is psychic. It's just that in a lot of people, their abilities have gone to sleep, buried beneath layers of dust from years of neglect and indoctrination about what is achievable and what isn't. With energy work, you will become even more aware of the energy centers, which will activate them. This, in turn, will cause you to experience psychic phenomena that relate to each unique one and will allow you to become a more spiritually evolved being. Not in the way that most people mean when they write that in their social media bio, but true spiritual evolution, the kind that reveals the many wonders that exist beyond this world.

The Energy Centers

All of these the energy centers we've glossed over before coming together to make up the energy body, and they're all connected to one another through an infinite number of energy paths. While you get the energy to your physical body by eating and drinking, you get subtle energy through your hands and feet, breath, environment, and all social interactions you have. When you take in life force, it moves through the various pathways and your energy centers, which work to convert that energy just like a transformer so it can serve your unique needs.

The primary energy centers are connected to your emotions. If you listen to music you love, you may feel a pleasant tingle that runs through your back. If you feel sad, you may notice that your body feels heavy and sluggish. If you receive shocking news, your chest can tighten, or your throat might go dry, and if you feel excited or afraid, goosebumps might suddenly pop up on your skin, causing your hair to stand. If it's a scary enough situation, your legs might even go weak. Your head might start bothering you if you feel tense or stressed out, or you might literally feel the ache in your chest if you suffer a heartbreak. Oppositely, if you feel love, you'll get butterflies in your stomach.

You may not have realized it until this point, but when you feel these things, that's your energy body making itself known to you. It's no accident you get these physical reactions to your emotions at those precise parts of your body. There are seven chakras:

- The base or root chakra
- The navel chakra
- The solar plexus chakra
- The heart chakra
- The throat chakra
- The brow or third eye chakra
- The crown chakra

We will cover each one in detail over the course of this book, but for now, you need to know these energy centers handle your emotions and your spiritual and psychic senses.

The secondary centers are smaller than the chakras, simpler in function, and vary in size. They're everywhere in your body, and you can find out more about them by studying the traditional acupuncture systems of the Chinese. With these centers, there are four poles and a core that connects them all. Think of each pole as a little cortex that rises up to the skin and sits right above the joint. The poles are connected through even bigger conduits, which pass through the marrow and middle of all your bones. When there's energy flowing strongly in the cores, you might notice tingling sensations, particularly in your legs and arms. These centers can be found in each joint of your body and other organs.

The tertiary centers are just like the many sweat pores you have, allowing you to swap energies with the people and environment around you. There are many of these all over your skin, but certain hotspots contain more than usual:

- Palms
- Soles of your feet
- Genitalia
- Ears

- Eyes
- Nose
- Nasal passages
- Lips
- Tongue
- Mouth

They have a high level of sensitivity. This is especially the case with your hands since they allow you to pick up on energy fields.

There are just three energy storage centers. The sub-navel center is halfway between your pubic line and belly button, about two inches into your body. It works to contain physical vitality. When you stimulate it, you'll feel bubbling or fluttering just an inch or two to the sides of the midpoint or your pubic line. This fluttering is by no means the same as what you get when you have gas.

Then there's the sub-heart center, which is between your nipples, right in the middle of your chest, also two inches deep in the average human body. Its job is to contain all emotional energy. Finally, you have the sub-brow center, which is smack dab in the middle of your brow, between your eyebrows, in the skull. Its role is to contain and disburse mental or psychic energy. It is imperative to note you must focus on keeping the sub-navel storage center full. When you do this, that energy will then bubble up to the sub-heart and sub-brow centers. There are many people too desperate to open their third eye chakras that ignore this warning. Remember that it often leads to terrible, unwanted side effects that can disrupt your emotional, psychic, and mental stability.

The central channel is a vertical one in the middle of your body, moving from the perineum or base chakra to the middle of the crown chakra to the top and middle of your head. It generates a field of energy that extends and balloons above your head. To the left of the Sushumna, you have the Ida conduit, while the Pingala conduit is on the right. Their roots move from your legs and go into the base chakra, weaving around the central channel as they go up while passing through each chakra. Your spine and spinal cord are tied to the central channel energetically, but the area where the central channel is taken up by the spine is more aligned with your head and torso. On the outside, it feels magnetic, and it rotates clockwise, then in the opposite direction. These rotational changes take anywhere from 10 minutes to a whole hour or longer, depending on the individual and the various changes in physical and mental conditions. It rotates more one way than the other, and if you're sensitive enough, you can pick up on the changes, which depend on energy flow through the legs. The legs take turns, dominating energy flow. When the other leg takes over, you might feel some disturbance as the Sushumna pauses, then turns the other way. It might feel like a bit of dizziness – if you notice it at all.

Your aura is also an important thing to discuss. The activity in your energy body generates it, and the distance it covers depends on the subtle one's health, activity level, and development. It's like an egg that encircles your physical body by about a yard. Each chakra sends colored energy into the field. We'll get into the colors later but combined, they form a connection in the aura. Most people will only see a general color, which depends on the present emotions and state of mind. You can see the aura either with clairvoyant sight or with aura sight. The latter involves using your eyes and brow chakra simultaneously, so you can see the colors superimposed on your usual vision. You need to look at the person with peripheral vision, looking slightly to their side and softening your focus. Then you hold your gaze until the aura shows up. Clairvoyance involves using your brow chakra alone, either with eyes open or shut. With this sight, you will see even more than just a general color.

Energy Exercise

This exercise is by Robert Bruce, the creator of the tactile imaging system of energy work. You will learn how to move your awareness around various parts of your body.

1. Grab a ruler (you might not need this).
2. Eliminate all distractions.
3. Sit in a chair. Keep your shoes off, legs uncrossed, clothing light, and loose.
4. Lightly scratch or rub a specific part of your body (pick your left knee, for starters). You should feel a tingle you can focus on.
5. Stop scratching and notice the tingle. Feel any change in temperature or air movement. Feel using your sense of touch in your mind.
6. Feel the sides and back of your knee, and then wrap your awareness around the entire knee a few times, just like you would a bandage.
7. Next, slowly move that awareness to your big toe. You may scratch it or wiggle it to help you focus on it. Feel its shape with your mind. Move your awareness through your big toe, back and forth, for just a minute.
8. Next, repeat the whole exercise with your right knee and toe.
9. Repeat this exercise with any part of your body you like, but it would be best if you move your awareness all over your body, remembering to notice the temperature and air changes.

You may feel some sensations, and that's okay. You're waking up your energy body. Now it's time to move on to tactile imaging.

1. Get rid of all distractions. Wear loose comfy clothing.

2. Sit in a quiet place, with your shoes off. Set a cushion beneath your feet and keep them uncrossed.

3. Shut your eyes and take a few settling breaths until you're lightly relaxed.

4. Raise your hand and comb your fingers through your hair. Notice what that feels like because you will recreate the sensations using just your awareness. Take as much time as you need.

5. Put your hand down and do this again, using just your awareness or "imaginary hand," if you will. Imagine combing your fingers through your hair and feel it on your scalp. Keep going until you've covered your whole scalp and the length of your hair.

6. Wrap up by using both of your imaginary hands now. Let them rise in your mind, and then massage your scalp, and then your face, shoulders, and neck. Do this slowly and keep your attention on the contact point between your hands and your body.

Chapter Two: Chakras and Colors

Chakras are the primary energy centers of the energy body. There are seven, at least according to the Hindu system, which is the most accepted one, seeing as it is complete than any other system out there. The chakras contain all your memories from the day you were born to right now. They determine how you interact with the world around you and what you value and desire the most.

Within a Chakra

Let's look at what the chakra is all about. First, know that each chakra has a Sanskrit name and other names based on the Vedas, Yoga, and the Puranas. They also have a specific position they occupy relative to your spine and other structures in the body. Every chakra has its very own purpose. Unique colors match their vibrational frequencies, and specific sounds, sound representatives, lotus numbers, cosmic planes, attributes, gods and goddesses, planets, psychic gifts, granthi, auric fields, and secondary chakras, among other factors. There will be times throughout your life when a specific one becomes active.

Each chakra is associated with an endocrine gland and manages specific physical organs or structures and processes in the body. There's always a physical sense and organ that is connected to each chakra, and they each have an action organ, which is the primary center of all the chakra's physical activity. Some handle a certain type of breath, and they all have particular illnesses that show a lack of energy flow to them. These illnesses will typically affect only the related body parts.

Your chakras all have parts to play when it comes to your thought patterns and your emotions. There are also certain Jungian archetypes linked to each one, meaning, your personality and self-expression depend on which chakra is most dominant in your energy body. Your character is also affected by the chakras that don't have enough energy flow. When there's too much energy running through the chakra, psychological effects occur. This is why balancing your chakra is fundamental. Each has its own symbol or yantra that works great for meditations to balance or open it.

Each chakra relates to an element, which is represented by certain sounds and colors. The elements are:

- Earth or prithvi
- Water or apas
- Air or vayu
- Fire or tejas
- Ether or panchabhuta

As you can probably tell, there is more to chakras than just colors and their locations in the subtle body.

The Origin of the Chakra System

The chakra system has been around since the period between 1500 and 500 BC in India. It was mentioned in the ancient spiritual text known as the Vedas. These energy centers are also mentioned in the Shri Jabala Darshana Upanishad, the Yoga-Shikha Upanishad, the Cudamini Upanishad, and the Shandilya Upanishad. All knowledge about these centers was also passed on from generation to generation by oral tradition among the Indo-Europeans. It was mainly an Eastern school of thought until Western authors wrote about the system, drawing from the ancient texts and making the knowledge easier to access for the rest of us.

The Structure of Chakras

The chakra has quite a lot to do with every level of your existence. Envision a vortex of light that reduces to a point like a tornado. If you could see it right now, you would notice the light that swirls like a wheel, moving either clockwise or counterclockwise. Slowed down, you would see that it's made up of vortexes that constitute a whirlpool of energy. The number of these vortexes varies from chakra to chakra. A completely still chakra looks just like a lotus's petals, which is why when you see drawings of them, they each have varying numbers of petals to represent the number of vortexes.

Imagine seven little tornadoes coming out the front and back of your body, making a total of fourteen. They are on the inside of the body, with these 14 projections to the outside. These flower-like vortexes narrow down to a point along the spine or in the head. They serve an important function of drawing Kundalini energy so you can feel healthy at all levels of your being and transform yourself spiritually.

Besides being stacked vertically along the spine and head, they each have a horizontal energy band that vibrates, extending from your body, perceived as both sound and color. It is supposed to handle whatever matches those bands of energy. They are set up so it denotes the vibrational level of physical or spiritual issues. The higher the chakra, the higher it is in vibration, and so the higher its effects, spiritually. This in no way suggests there is something wrong about the "low" chakras, for the root is just as divine as the crown and any other chakra.

The lower chakras help you develop as a fully healthy person on Earth, while the higher ones help you develop as a spiritual being. These centers work to balance the masculine and feminine, the Yin and Yang in your life. They make sure that the energy is balanced on both sides of the body, with the left being feminine and the recipient of energy and the right being masculine, transmitting that same energy.

The Aura

The aura is an electromagnetic field you generate through the bioelectricity that is the outcome of all activity in your body. So, your aura is a body of light that surrounds the physical one. This light is given off in seven layers, which all relate to various aspects of your health—spiritually, mentally, emotionally, and physically. These layers can all work with one another to create the desired effect on your health. With clairvoyant or auric sight, you can see them and any issues that might be lurking within them.

If you've ever thought of auras as being like "vibes," then you're not far off the mark. The aura, after all, comprises energy at various vibrational frequencies. Depending on the vibe, you can tell when someone is upset or ecstatic without him or her having to express or say anything about how they feel. You can also read their actual feelings through the aura because while words and facial expressions can be carefully set up to tell a story, the aura never lies.

Every living thing has its own field of energy. As humans, we have more evolved, more complex energy fields. We're basically like biological radio stations, broadcasting our vibes and receiving the vibes of everything around us in turn.

What the Aura Looks Like

There are those who say that the aura depends on the medium used to capture it. We've already talked about viewing it using clairvoyant and auric sight, but you can also use a special camera to see the aura of anyone. This photography is known as Kirlian photography. Thanks to this, there is definitive proof that the aura is indeed shaped like an egg and surrounds the entire physical body. Artistically, it is depicted as a light bubble or a halo that surrounds the body.

How to See Your Aura

You probably don't have a special camera lying around to see your aura, but you can still see it by looking at yourself in the mirror, making sure that the wall behind you is a uniform, solid color (preferably white), and then softening your gaze while you look at your reflection. You want to keep your attention on your brow chakra, which is in the middle and just above the eyes as you do this. You don't look right at yourself, but to the areas at the sides of your head. Breathe in a deep and relaxed way, and you will see your aura. You want to beware of the color of clothing you're wearing; something too bright might affect what you see, so either try this in your birthday suit or wear a solid, simple color like grey, black, or white. Remember, to keep your gaze soft, look at yourself through your peripheral vision. Don't be in a rush. If you see nothing after ten to fifteen minutes, you can imagine seeing a glow around you the next time you try this exercise. Imagination is a great way to stimulate your third eye, so it wakes up and becomes more sensitive to your aura and other things you rarely perceive.

Aura Colors

Each layer of the aura has its own color, brighter in people who are naturally vibrant and have high energy and duller in those who are physically unwell, emotionally down, or going through a lot of stress. There's no reason to be concerned if the aura has no color, and you should also keep in mind that colors tend to change with time. Naturally, each auric layer lines up with the chakras of your body. Certain layers are more pronounced than others, revealing the most dominant chakra.

Each color has its own meaning. Red says you're full of energy, have a strong will, and are grounded. Orange implies that you're a considerate person who's always thoughtful and open to adventure. Yellow shows that you're generally friendly, highly creative, and usually relaxed and at ease. Green says you have great communication skills, which lend themselves to your ability to socialize freely. You also have a nurturing spirit. Blue means you're a spiritual freethinker who relies heavily on intuition and is rarely ever led astray. Indigo suggests that you're gentle, very in touch with your spiritual side, and you stay curious about life. Violet implies great wisdom and intellect and a fiercely independent spirit.

The Kundalini

The Kundalini — Sanskrit for "life energy" — is a subtle energy that lies within the body, activating the chakras and leading to your spiritual development. Sometimes called the rainbow serpent or the red serpent, it helps to fuel your chakras with energy, keep you in good health, and, if you let it, take you on the path to spiritual enlightenment. It is described as a serpent coiled at the bottom of the root chakra, around the coccyx. This feminine energy remains dormant until you wake it up, and then it uncoils and springs upwards, moving through all energy channels to get the energy to all seven chakras. Its destination is the crown chakra, which is masculine. It allows you to unify all levels of yourself, to attain at-one-ment.

Some people are born with an already active Kundalini, while others have theirs naturally expand. It could also arise because of something traumatizing or years of spiritual work like meditation, yoga, and energy work. You could also get an energy master to help you activate your Kundalini.

Some people will experience an awakening within the first chakra, which comes with sudden sexual desire, security crises, hot flashes, emotional issues, and body shakes. Unfortunately, many people remain stuck at that level for many years. There are others who experience Kundalini rising easily, quickly moving through all the chakras. No matter how it plays out, it's different for everyone. When you have activated your Kundalini, you will feel like you're full of energy and at peace simultaneously. With some people, Kundalini activation also comes with various psychic gifts called siddhi in Hindu. As you work through your chakras, you'll learn of your Kundalini energy and know what to do with it when the time comes.

Chapter Three: The Root Chakra - Muladhara

The root chakra is also called Muladhara and is right at the bottom of your reproductive organs and anus. It sits at the bottom of the spinal column in the perineum area. That is where the Kundalini — the shakti power of change — lies coiled, asleep. It is connected to the ida, Pingala, and Sushumna and is connected to all matters of survival, safety, security, and physical needs.

This center is red, and it is called the root chakra because it roots you into your identity, ancestry, and everyday life. It is this chakra that allows you to exist, to heal, and to manifest your desired reality. Because of this, we become who we are, make love, work, and breathe. While it is the very seat of Kundalini and represents the fire energy of sex, driving all desire, it is also the epitome of innocence. It depicts a childlike ecstasy that allows you to have dignity and honor, showing you to trust the Divine for all your needs, no matter what you're going through.

The Muladhara's Qualities

Muladhara comprises the Sanskrit words mul (meaning "base") and adhara (meaning "support"). The function of this chakra is to root us and sustain us every day.

At the base of the spine, it is related to the sacrococcygeal nerve plexus. Some say this chakra is between the scrotum and anus in men, while it is near the cervix's posterior portion in women. The Sat-Cakra Nirupana says it's four fingers in width and sits two-fingers below the genitals and above the anus.

Right above the Muladhara is the Kundalini chakra, which is just where the Sushumna and the Muladhara meet. The latter's four petals cover each of the Kundalini chakra's four sides.

Your spinal cord finishes like a fine thread, and a strand of fibrous tissue (non-neural in nature) known as the filum terminale, which works to support the cord. This same strand moves down from the tapered end of your spinal cord called the conus medullaris and is made of an upper and lower part. The upper part, being 15 centimeters long, extends toward the lower portion of your second sacral vertebra, and that lower portion is connected to the posterior section of the coccyx's first segment. Muladhara is right at the bottom of the filum terminale.

Muladhara is connected to your perineum, hips, and bladder and affects your legs and feet as it roots you to the Earth. It is this chakra that powers your body energetically. If you're low on energy, struggling with financial problems, faced with a life-or-death crisis, and even other bodily issues, this is the chakra to concern yourself with first.

This chakra oversees your physical energies. It gives you the drive to preserve yourself. Again, its basic color is red, which is also the color of Shakti, the goddess who represents awakening, movement, and energy. It has a secondary color, black, which represents matter.

According to the Hindu chakra system, it becomes active anywhere from age one to age seven. This process shows itself in the basic motivations associated with this energy center, like drinking, eating, and sleeping. Typically, it is necessary for the child to be self-centered at this age, as this confirms that the child will survive.

This chakra is connected to the adrenals, which are two little organs that sit right on top of your kidneys. The function of the adrenals gives a bit of clarity about the role of the root chakra. These adrenals are also called stress glands for a good reason; when you're stressed out, they'll pump out hormones that respond to the stress.

Body Parts

This root chakra handles various parts of the body, including the bones, muscles, bladder, rectum, hip joints, immune system, coccygeal vertebrae, and lower extremities. It also handles the large intestine, the process of elimination, parts of the genitals, and the prostate and kidneys.

Major Sense

The Muladhara oversees the sense of smell and the nose.

Action Organ

Your feet are the active organs of this center.

Vital Breath

Apana is one of the five essential pranas of the base chakra that also handles exhalation, elimination of toxins, digestive waste, and menstruation.

Related Illnesses

When the root chakra is out of balance, you might struggle with eating disorders and obesity. Other troubling health conditions that could arise include constipation, fibromyalgia, sciatica, hemorrhoids, chronic fatigue, and issues with the feet, knees, and legs. An out-of-balance Muladhara also leads to skin issues, arthritis, varicose veins, teeth and bone disorders, issues with the anus, large intestine, and bowels, problems with the base of your spine, issues with drug and alcohol addiction, reproduction problems, and blood deficiencies.

Psychological Issues

Your root chakra handles all beliefs and feelings that lend themselves to how secure and safe you are in life. The central idea of this chakra is that you exist, and you deserve to. Every primal feeling you have, including the raw emotions of fear, anger, disgust, sadness, and joy, are processed by this specific one. It also processes reactions like rage, futility, resentment, abandonment, terror, despair, oneness, bliss, guilt, shame, and longing.

When your beliefs are supportive of your entire self — including your spiritual side — then it's easy for you to manifest the love, money, and health you seek. When you're unaware of whom you are, you will feel like you're unworthy, unwanted, and undeserving of the good things of life. This leads to feelings of lack, unhappiness, dissatisfaction, and so on.

All your early childhood issues and past life karma are wrapped up in the Muladhara, and it is all this that determines the amount of joy or sadness you go through in your present life. Sure, you may not be able to do anything about your past karma other than balance it out, but you are responsible for your present life's karma. The way to make sure this karma is positive is by learning to remain in control of your mind and senses by choosing discipline every time.

The traumas that affect the root chakra include challenges with money or giving birth, sexual and physical abuse, addiction, and feeling unloved and unwanted by our parents and loved ones. If this center is not balanced, you'll notice you can't manifest your desires, you don't feel grounded, and you feel very disconnected from society. You could also suffer anxiety and depression. If you've ever run across someone full of blame, hatred, resentment, and hurt, then they do not have a balanced root chakra.

Archetypes

Muladhara is tied to the Mother archetype. According to Carl Jung, the Mother represents the transcendence of logic and reason by spirit, the magic of feminine authority, instinct, growth, and maternal sympathy. This chakra also has the negative archetype, which is the Victim. This is something to be aware of because it means someone could use you for his or her personal gain, and at the same time, be likely to assume that your problems aren't your fault.

Personality

People who are gifted when it comes to Muladhara are very materialistic. They would rather focus on their basic, material needs before turning their attention to other people. For them, success is about creating and building resources they can continue to tap into. They are strong in character, full of stamina, and have a passion for the physical world.

Excesses and Deficiencies

When the first chakra is deficient, you'll feel disconnected and spaced out. People who have no balance in this center might be a tad underweight, suffer from anxiety and crippling fear, have issues focusing or following through on what they set out to achieve, and have self-destructive tendencies. They may feel like they are unlovable, have no idea what healthy boundaries are, might be masochistic and even suicidal, generally passive, and lack financial abundance.

People with an overactive first chakra are often overweight, suffer from paranoia and hypochondria, and spend more money than they have. They also love to hoard things, can be greedy, lazy, and fatigue easily. They resist change because they're afraid of it and would rather have their clear boundaries with security and no room for flexibility.

Balanced Muladhara

When this chakra is balanced, you experience true security, prosperity, and ease in your body. You will find yourself fully grounded, full of energy, in complete control of your body. You say yes to adventure, manifest what you need, and remain calm no matter what's going on.

Exercise to Open and Balance This Chakra

1. Sit or stand somewhere quiet. Make sure no one will bother you while you do this exercise and that distractions like cell phones are turned off.

2. Imagine a beam of light moving from the top of your head right through your spine at the bottom and down to the Earth's center. This beam of light is the grounding cord.

3. Imagine that there's a white light projected from the sky right into the grounding cord. See this white light encasing the cord.

4. Understand that energy from the sky will move all negative energies into the Earth's center, where they will be transmuted.

5. As you start to feel clean thanks to the light, let your inner self or spirit self-sense the elements from Earth you need for healthy physical and energetic bodies. The classical elements are Earth, ether, fire, water, and air. Other elements are metal, stone, light, wood, and star energy.

6. As you feel yourself being filled by these energies, allow yourself to notice how calm, refreshed, and present you are. Relax and allow these elements to nourish and replenish you. You might notice that you're drawn to certain elements more than others. This is fine. Allow it.

7. In your peaceful state, ask your higher self what you must think about right now and what you should do with the wisdom you receive from this contemplation.

8. Consider the intentions you would like to set and how your resolutions will help you discover or express yourself as whom you are.

9. Set an intention to get rid of all doubt and false ideas you might have about the things you deserve in life, including love and wealth.

10. Seek the support of the Divine or your higher self in helping you discover all that you are.

11. Take deep, long, loving breaths, and ask your higher self to help you so you always are cleansed by the white light and supported by the Earth.

Muladhara Yantra

The yantra or symbol for this chakra is a yellow square, set in the middle of four red petals, with eight spears, which signify all directions. In the square is a triangle with its top point down, and within is the symbol for the seed. Close to or above the seed is the Brahma as a child, red with four arms and faces. In Brahma's three hands, he has a rosary, gourd, and staff. In his one empty hand, he makes the gesture that banishes all fear.

Also present is the red Shakti Dakini, with four arms in which he holds a drinking cup, sword, skull-staff, and spear. A white elephant is at the triangle's lower point. The yantra also has the Kundalini, which is wrapped around the Shiva lingam three and a half times.

The triangle or trikona represents the Kundalini in its dormant state and the female energy – or yoni. It points downward because at this energy center, you're only getting started with your spiritual development, and the more you grow, the more your enlightenment climbs up and out, just like the top of the triangle.

The Shiva lingam is male energy that represents creativity, and the serpent's head points down to show you can either evolve or devolve. The snake also represents the past, present, and future.

Parts of the Muladhara

Its gross element is Earth, while its subtle element is smell or attraction. Its color is yellow, while its sound is Lam, which represents spiritual awakening. Lam is connected to the king of the gods named Indra, who defends all men against the force of evil.

Muladhara has the attributes of both greed and patience. Its sound carrier is the seven-trunked elephant, or airavata, a sign of wisdom and abundance and carries the creator god Brahma. It gives wealth to whoever has it, and its brain is beyond valuable. The seven trunks represent the body's seven basic materials, and the Earth's seven precious gems and minerals. It also represents all levels of consciousness:

- Unconsciousness
- Subconsciousness
- Dream consciousness
- Astral consciousness
- Waking consciousness
- Cosmic consciousness
- Supreme consciousness

The root chakra's lotus is called mula kamala. It has four petals representing the mind, consciousness, intellect, ego, and the North, South, East, and West. They also represent the various stages of life on the planet: vegetation, oviparous animals, mammals, and humans. Each petal is red with a gold letter stamped on it. The four letters on the petals are sa, va, sha, and sha.

Cosmic Plane

This chakra's cosmic plane is called bhu loka. There are seven underworlds that exist just beneath the Muladhara, and they are connected to the minor energy centers found in the limbs, controlled by the root chakra.

Gods and Goddesses

Dakini, the one who acts as reality's gatekeeper, rules this chakra. You also have the goddesses Devi Shakti (a creative force) and Asuri Shakti (a destructive one). By doing good and only spending time with those who are good, we can transmute all Asuri into Devi. Brahma is the god connected to this chakra, the one who rules all of physicality. You also have the god Ganesh, who gets rid of obstacles and offers protection, and Lord Shiva, who oversees animals and teaches us how to keep our base instincts in check. This chakra's planet is Saturn, which shows you how to handle your limits.

Granthi or Knot

Granthi is the various phases through which Kundalini must go to lead to ascension. Brahma's knot or Brahma granthi needs to be untied so that you can set yourself free from all thoughts that have you thinking the Earth is a prison. It represents the resistance we all have to change. Once you undo this knot, your Kundalini can rise to the next level.

Psychic Abilities or Siddhis

Siddhis are supernatural powers, and certain ones that come with this chakra include strength, mastery over five senses, and mastery over all things on Earth and other matters. You might also find that your jumps are as powerful as a frog's and that you have amazing control of your breath, thoughts, and even semen. You will find when it is balanced, it can allow you to be completely free of sickness, teach you to dominate all esoteric matters, get everything you desire, and enjoy a blissful state of being.

You gain other psychic abilities with a well-balanced and active root chakra, including:

- Clairgustance (or clear tasting)
- Clairtangency (the ability to touch things that aren't in the room)
- Cleromancy (a method of divination)
- Feng shui (mastery over the environment)
- Dowsing (finding objects in the ground)
- Psychometry (learning about something or someone through touch)
- And – of course – telekinesis (moving things around using your mind)

You can use these gifts to levitate things, shift from one dimension to the next, start fires using just your mind, as well as healing people energetically.

Auric Layer

The first auric layer is connected to the Muladhara. This layer is right outside your skin. If you could see it with auric sight, you'd notice it penetrates your skin and extends outwards all over your body by 1-½ inches.

Exercise: The Nasikagra Drishti or Agochari Mudra

This exercise is about you gazing at your nose tip until you begin to pick up on psychic fragrances.

1. Sit in a comfy, quiet place, and gaze right ahead, breathing as usual. You want your shoulders relaxed and your palms comfortably positioned on your knees.

2. Move your eyes slowly until the tip of your nose is in sight. You want to hold that gaze just for a few seconds while holding your breath. If you start to feel any discomfort or pain, shift your gaze back to normal.

3. Repeat this often during a session, for as long as you can hold that gaze each time, returning to your normal gaze, so you don't strain your eyes terribly. Practice this for a month to see if you are better at sensing smells when you're thinking of someone or thinking about an experience you had.

Secondary Chakras

There are seven of these beneath the root, all going down the legs. They are also known as talas, which have corresponding lokas, psychic spheres. While the talas are shadowy in form, the lokas are luminous. Here are the talas you should concern yourself with:

- The atala, located in the hips, governs lust and fear.
- The vitala, located in the thighs, deals with resentment and anger.
- The sutala, located in the knees, deals with jealousy.
- The talatala in the calves controls willful tendencies and extended bouts of confusion.
- The rasatala in the ankles controls our animalistic nature and selfishness.
- The mahatala in the feet oversees the dark realm, the consciousness with no conscience, and inner, spiritual blindness.
- The patella in the soles of your feet deals with torture, malice, murder, hell, and hatred.

The root chakra is the very foundation of your life. The Kundalini lies coiled, waiting to rise. This chakra will give you a sense of safety and security you need as it oversees your important life and death processes.

Chapter Four: The Sacral Chakra - Svadisthana

Svadisthana is the chakra that's right above Muladhara. This chakra symbolizes life's sacred waters, which nourish us and connect us with the people that matter the most to us.

The Svadisthana's Qualities

Svadisthana comprises two Sanskrit words, sva meaning "self" and adhisthana meaning "residence, seat, or dwelling place." Therefore, this chakra is the dwelling place of self. You can find it sitting three inches away from the Muladhara, on top, right between the sacrum and coccyx, and about 2 inches beneath the navel.

Svadisthana oversees our creativity, emotions, and sensual nature. It is orange, which is the same as the rising sun and consciousness as it ascends. Energetically, this color communicates purity, action, energy, faith, and joy. According to the Hindu chakra system, Svadisthana becomes active from age seven to fourteen, when kids at this age find they need about eight hours a night to sleep (ten hours, max), usually in a fetal position. At this stage, Muladhara's Earth becomes Svadisthana water, where bonds between family and friends are created in a healthy environment, fostering creativity.

The ovaries are related to this center in women, while it's the testes for men. Sure, the prostate gland is often associated with the first chakra, but some systems say it's also connected to the second.

Body Parts

Svadisthana oversees all the body's sexual organs, including the cervix, uterus, and vagina. It also oversees the pelvis, the appendix, lower vertebrae, upper intestines, parts of the digestive organs, and kidneys.

Major Sense

The major sense organ is the tongue, so the sense of this center is taste.

Action Organ

The genitals are the active organs of this center.

Vital Breath

Prana is the vital breath of this chakra.

Related Illnesses

When you have issues with your second chakra, you might have problems with your urinary and reproductive systems. You may also need to deal with sexual dysfunction, menstrual issues, constant lower back pain, joint issues, sciatica, appendicitis, no sensual pleasure, every itis that affects the bowels, and an addiction to carbohydrates.

Psychology

This energy center is what starts and keeps up the bond we share with others. A lot of these connections inevitably are emotional, and they work as the bedrock of all relationships, healthy and otherwise. It is this chakra that connects our emotional reactions to the emotional attachments we form.

Thanks to this chakra, we can connect with our sensual side, which is a huge part of our identity, allowing us to connect with others of the same sex or a different one from ours. The fantasies you entertain and the moods you allow yourself to dwell in can create extreme fluctuations, especially when there is a struggle with the natural love for pleasure, our desires, and acting on them.

Without proper self-care, it's possible to allow Svadisthana to cause us to think less of ourselves or even give in to abusing others. As the Kundalini becomes active, it's possible to generate greed, jealousy, envy, and rage, unless we tend to the beliefs that foster resentment, fear, and prejudice within us. This chakra demands you learn of your shadow self and develop the discipline and strength required to be watchful, so it doesn't take over completely. You have to come to the place where you accept that others love you, and you can trust and allow your emotions to steer you down the right path.

Archetypes

The positive archetype of the second chakra is that of the Empress or Emperor. Carl Jung describes this as the ruler within you and your ability to make your desires come to pass. This center's negative archetype is the Martyr, who revels in suffering because it's a gateway to pity and attention. Transmuted, this archetype also allows you to devote your life to a sacred, worthy cause.

Personality

Those who are blessed with an active second chakra are emotionally sensitive. They are often the heart of whatever they're a part of, unafraid to express themselves, display a lot of creativity that comes easily to them, and want nothing more than to be remembered for something unique by the world. They are empaths that connect with others on an emotional level, sometimes to the point of neglecting their own needs to take care of other people. When they do take the reins of their own sensual desires, emotions, and values, they're in a better position of strength to be compassionate.

Excesses and Deficiencies

When there is a deficiency in the Svadisthana, the body becomes rigid. The same thing happens with beliefs. The deficient second chakra leads to a crippling fear of the new and change, self-denial, zero social skills, the squelching of desire, and a lack of creativity. When it's in excess, there's the matter of addiction to many things like shopping, sex, substances, romance, carbs, and even wine. Excesses also lead to irresponsible behavior, living life based on emotions, manipulation through deliberate seduction, invasiveness, lack of respect for boundaries, attachment to things and people that borders on obsession, and codependency.

Balanced Svadisthana

The balanced sacral chakra allows you to enjoy sensuality, friendliness, vitality, satisfaction, sexual expression, compassion, and wonderful bonds with others.

Svadisthana Yantra

This center's yantra has a silver crescent in it, which represents the moon. The moon is nestled in a white circle reminiscent of water. This shows the relationship between the moon and water. The moon affects you in so many ways as it moves through all its phases. Svadisthana, being connected to the genitals, is a symbol of procreation. This same heavenly body even affects the process of menstruation. Within the yantra, you also find Brahma as the cosmic egg or the golden womb that births all knowledge and the goddess Rakini.

Parts of the Svadisthana

The Svadisthana has the gross element of water. Its subtle element is taste and/or attraction. The element's color is light blue, white, or transparent, much like water, while its sound is Vam, which is the embodiment of the aspect of Vishnu known as Varuna. This is the center to which attachment and purity belong. The crocodile represents sexual vigor and sensuality, also called makara. This is easy to understand because the crocodile is lethargic one moment and violently active the next. Within Svadisthana, there is the laziness displayed by this creature while it watches its prey and the sudden surprise attack it's known for. This represents our ability to either be deceitful about our desire or choose to be emotionally available and transparent. The crocodile is a symbol for the lord of the waters called Varuna.

The second chakra has six petals that all connect to their own nadi. They represent the six vrittis of non-empathy, delusion, suspicion, disdain, destructiveness, and indulgence, all of which we need to work through and get rid of to allow ourselves to spiritually mature.

Exercise for Opening and Balancing This Chakra

Water and the moon are connected. You have only to notice the way the ocean's tides are affected by the moon. Similarly, the moon affects your body and its chemistry and connects you with the heavens.

For at least sixteen minutes each hour, you breathe through the left nostril, which activates the lunar ida nadi. This same nadi affects the right portion of your brain, which handles creativity, emotion, and intuition. As you breathe this way, you naturally will call forth the energy of the moon.

To be more intentional about left nostril breathing, try this exercise, which will not only cool your body down but keep it alkalized. The nose matters a lot for keeping your chakras and physical body in balance, as this organ is connected to the hypothalamus through the olfactory lobe. The hypothalamus is the part of your brain that tells you to fight, flee, or freeze in the face of danger or stressors. It's also super important when it comes to your sacral chakra.

As you breathe through your left nostril only, you will allow yourself to enjoy music, be charitable in all you do, offer to be of service, be better in your partnerships and friendships, and so on. More than simply enjoying these things, you will receive benefits in your life. So, here's how to carry out this exercise:

1. Sit comfortably, and then use a finger or two to block your right nostril.
2. Breathe in through the left one.
3. Exhale through the right.
4. Repeat this for at least one minute. You can go on for three minutes, tops.

    If you know that you've got heart disease or high blood pressure, please do not do this alternate nose breathing exercise.

Exercise to Increase Prana Flow to the Second Chakra

1. Sit in a comfortable position, in a quiet place where you won't be disturbed or distracted.
2. You're going to chant "vam." Keep your lips in a circle and then push out the air through them as you would into a tube.

3. As you do this, imagine your second chakra.

4. Continue to chant vam.

   As you chant, you will encourage more prana to flow to the chakra, and all insecurities you feel surrounding matters connected to the Svadisthana will melt away. You can also do this chant with the other seed sounds that represent the six petals:

- Bam (bham)
- Mam
- Yam
- Lam
- Ram

   As you chant, you will clear out the chakra and up your energy levels as well.

Cosmic Plane

The cosmic plane of this energy center is the astral plane or bhuvar loka.

Gods and Goddesses

Rakini or Chakini Shakti rules. She's a goddess with two heads and four arms, and, sitting on a red lotus, she holds an arrow, a drum, a skull, and an ax. She is one of the various representations of Kundalini Shakti, and her heads are the depiction of the second chakra's split energy, the "I versus the other." This goddess inspires all art and music.

Another goddess of note is Sarasvati, who is both wife and daughter of Brahma. Sarasvati turns Brahma's consciousness into actual knowledge. Brahma is also connected to this chakra as the creator of all knowledge or the "golden womb." In his place, Vishnu is also seen as a relevant god, dealing with matters of preservation. He symbolizes the importance of dealing with your Kundalini deliberately, using the breath. This chakra is ruled by Pluto, which is known for transformation. It also has no granthi or knot.

Exercise

For you to clear this chakra and enjoy the benefits, start with any meditation you like, whether it's a calm walk or easy focus on the breath. As you meditate, visualize the following:

1. Imagine seeing reflections of the moon in the water.

2. Allow the psychic, feminine, lunar energy to fill you as the water washes over you in a steady rhythm.

3. Allow all fluid within you to flow, so it restores you.

4. Chant the mantra vam repeatedly, as you feel all the nadis connected to this chakra open up to receive light and healing. This allows you to turn your anger, lust, jealousy, and greed into peace, compassion, and understanding.

5. Imagine Brahma opening up a door that leads to pure consciousness for you.

6. Imagine Rakini's ax chopping away all that is untrue and doesn't serve you from your soul.

7. Feel her drum as it beats in a restorative rhythm, bringing you back to balance.

8. Feel her spear separating vices like delusion and disdain from you.

9. See her skull as she holds it up to your face. Stare into it and allow yourself to see your romantic side. As you investigate this skull, feel yourself being set free from all fear of death.

Psychic Abilities

According to Tantric texts, when you master this chakra, you have nothing to fear from your enemies. You're like the Sun, with not a bit of darkness in you, set free from ignorance. Your words are imbued with wisdom, and they flow unimpeded. You have no fear of water, and you receive certain abilities, along with mastery over your five senses. You gain knowledge about all astral beings thanks to your mastery of Svadisthana, and you also have within you the ability to eradicate all that is impure. Master this chakra, and you defeat death.

With mastery comes gifts connected to emotions, like clairempathy (knowing exactly how someone or a particular situation feels or felt), claircognizance (also called clear knowing), clairgustance (or clear tasting), clairsentience (or clear sensing), and clairtangency (picking up on energy from things you are close to or can touch).

Auric Layer

The second auric layer is on top of the first, five inches above your skin surface. As for secondary chakras, there are none with this center.

Chapter Five: The Solar Plexus Chakra - Manipura

The Manipura is the third stop along the Kundalini's path. It draws in the prana your body needs to function, and it also has nadis that work to control digestion and other processes in the body.

Think of the Manipura as being your body's brain because it helps you gain wisdom, tap into intuition, and lend willpower to your thoughts, so you end up walking along with the Divine Plan for your life. This center connects both body and mind so that they act in tandem with each other and under the beliefs you hold. As you deal with the prejudices and fears that are a natural part of life and battle with your ego, you'll find there is a fire within you that shines brilliantly. If you allow this light to shine, then you will achieve success in all its forms. This means you need to have a balanced and working Manipura.

The Manipura's Qualities

Manipura comes from the Sanskrit words mani, meaning "gem or jewel," and pura, meaning "dwelling place." So, this energy center is the city of jewels. You can find it in the solar plexus, specifically, the bit of the vertebral column right behind the stomach. You can feel its energy exactly seven centimeters away from the navel, both above and below. Whenever you're stressed out, it can manifest as a tight knot just beneath your sternum. This energy center is yellow, which is a symbol of intellect and wisdom.

The Manipura's job is to serve as the store of your personal power. It's the place where your willpower comes from and what drives your mental activity and self-esteem. Some Tantric texts argue that Kundalini activation begins not in the Muladhara but the Manipura. These texts say that the first two chakras are just the higher planes of our animalistic selves and that human consciousness begins with the Manipura.

Since the third chakra is much higher than the first two, practitioners say that when your Kundalini rises to that point, you can't possibly head back down in consciousness. The only way to move is upwards and onwards. A few argue this is not the case, and it's possible for the Kundalini to drop back down to the Muladhara, even if it was as high as the crown chakra. Regardless of which school of thought you follow, the fact remains that the Manipura is crucial to raising your Kundalini.

Typically, Manipura is activated between ages 14 and 21 – around the time most people are driven to figure out who they are and how they want the world to see them. This is a time that could either result in bountiful service to others or great sorrow.

Body Parts

This chakra is connected to the pancreas. It's in charge of the digestive system, breath, skin, diaphragm, upper abdomen, small intestines, middle spine, parts of the adrenals and kidneys, including the adrenal cortex.

Manipura and your pancreas are connected, and so any issues with the pancreas could mean the Manipura is out of balance, or vice versa. To figure out the relationship between these two, you need to consider your pancreas' location. When it's where it should be, there will be a pulsing sensation right in the middle of your navel. If you have issues with anxiety, fatigue, diarrhea, pain in the stomach, and headaches, then it's possible you've got a displaced pancreas.

When the pulse that should be in your navel's middle is above it and to the left, you might have disorders affecting respiration. When it's to the left, you might struggle with emotions. To the right implies you have energy blockages, while below and to the right of your navel means you have digestive issues. When you breathe through the right nostril, you can bring this chakra back into balance and move your pancreas to where it should be. You can also use mantras to help balance this chakra.

Exercise

The Manipura is where words come from, which means it will respond to sound. You will discover how true this is by performing this exercise:

1. Put your thumb on your navel, then say any word aloud.

2. As you say this word, notice the vibration that bubbles at your navel before the words leave your lips.

3. Say the word again and feel the vibration moving from your navel to your larynx before the word comes out of your mouth.

4. Rather than a random word, you can use the mantra "ram." You may also chant om shanti so you can clear out your Manipura.

Om is the Divine sound, while shanti means "peace." Also, try chanting om mani padme hum, which translates to "my adoration to the master of the jeweled city." As you chant these, you will feel less tension within you, and your Manipura will become active and balanced.

Major Sense

The major sense with this center is sight, and the eyes are the sense organs.

Action Organ

The anus is the action organ.

Vital Breath

Samana is the vital breath that also cranks up your digestion.

Related Illnesses

When there are issues with the third chakra, expect problems with the digestive system, pancreatitis, diabetes, adrenal imbalance, kidney issues, some colon diseases, and low blood pressure. You may also have issues with food or digestion-related disorders like bulimia and anorexia, stomach ulcers, heartburn, chronic fatigue, hepatitis, hypoglycemia, muscular disorders, and leaky gut syndrome.

Psychology

The Manipura is where your personal power is, which will depend strongly on your emotions and beliefs that your ego holds on to. This is the center that helps you figure out your place, how valuable you are, and your ability to act on your decisions — preferably based on selfless sacrifice and not dharma or our past karma.

When blocked, you get anger, pride, victimization, prejudice, and fear. It also leads to being overly critical of everyone else or being too sensitive to handle criticism yourself. This situation allows you to be open to emotional manipulation, with you as the victim or someone else suffering this fate at your hands. You need to understand that while it is possible to manipulate ideas and people, the end of this path will give you no more than very troubling control issues and an over-inflated sense of self-worth.

Archetypes

This center's positive archetype is called the Warrior, which gives a power source second to none, one that can help you attain greatness when you channel it to worthy causes and make a difference in life. The negative archetype is called the Servant who serves all except herself, often because she seeks to be praised or recognized for her efforts. When used for good, this archetype can also allow you to strive towards better service to empower yourself.

Personality

When your Manipura is strong, you are quite the thinker. You love to play in the world of information, data, facts, ideas, and concepts. You organize this into a very understandable, workable system. You're an amazing administrator, and you can create the needed structures to achieve your goals or someone else's.

Excesses and Deficiencies

When this energy center has deficiencies, issues like low self-confidence and self-esteem, unhappiness, contraction in energy, poor digestion, and a lack of self-discipline show up. You're open to being manipulated with a deficient Manipura, and you might find yourself being passive, choosing to blame others, adopting a victim mindset, and proving generally unreliable. With excesses, you have issues with aggression, domination, a need to be right, a desire to always be in control, pride, egotism, hyperactivity, and competition.

Balanced Manipura

When all is balanced, you can assert yourself in healthy ways while remaining very cooperative. Your energy is dynamic. You are swift and clear with your decisions; your productivity reaches peak levels, you're intelligent and demonstrate focus in thought. Your body digests food as it should, you're in great shape and healthy, and for working, you're doing well and are happy with your circumstances.

Manipura Yantra

The yantra has a triangle that points down and is enclosed in a circle. At each side of the triangle is a T-shaped figure, which, when put together, all create a swastika. The actual meaning of the swastika is global welfare and wellbeing. It means good luck, no matter what direction the legs of these Ts are bent toward, and even when they're straight. The swastika is also a symbol of fire's nature, as it is the element of transformation.

Exercise to Open and Balance Manipura

The Manipura is just like the sun, bursting into brightness as the Kundalini and prana unite. Your right nostril is connected with the nadi of your Pingala, linked to the brain's left hemisphere, which deals with the logical, rational, physical, and verbal activities, and is masculine. With right nostril breathing, body heat and acidity go up. Normally, you switch from left nostril breathing to right nostril breathing. When you choose to breathe through the right nostril, you will fire up all chakras with a fiery nature, like Manipura. This exercise is also great for writing, going hard at your work, taking on debates, and deepening your spiritual practice.

1. Sit in a comfy chair.
2. Use a finger or two to block your left nostril.
3. Breathe in through the right nostril.
4. Exhale through the left.
5. Do this for one minute, at least, or three minutes tops.

    Please do not do this exercise if you're dealing with heart disease or high blood pressure.

Parts of the Manipura

Manipura's main element is fire. This is connected to the Hindu idea that all heat is what makes digestion possible, and so food and information are burned to create life force. The subtle element of this chakra is sight or form. This element's color is fire red, while its sound is the ram.

It has the attributes of supremacy and achievement. The sound carrier, ram, encourages everything spiritual by offering you strength, bravery, and wisdom. The fire god, Agni, shows the value of steadfastness and never giving up.

Manipura has ten petals, all blue, just like the blue you'd find in the middle of a hot flame. This means it's both creative and destructive. Each petal signifies treachery, spiritual ignorance, delusion, shame, jealousy, foolishness, fear, disgust, sadness, and thirst.

This center belongs to the celestial plane, also called svar loka or heaven. Its ruling goddess is Lakini Shakti, who is also called Bhadra Kali. This is Kali in her compassionate form. She has three faces, which show that her vision is broad. Her four arms hold an arrow, fire, a thunderbolt, and a mudra, which grants blessings and dispels all fear.

The ruling god is Old Shiva or Rudra. This is the version of Shiva, who is full of wrath, and symbolizes destructive power. The name Rudra comes from the root word rud or "crying," which happens in mourning of an ending. While Rudra is red because of the anger he feels, he is also gray or white due to the ashes that cover his body while he sits on a tiger skin, holding on to a drum and a trident. Rudra, adorned with serpents, banishes both anger and fear. The ruling planet of Manipura is the Sun, which represents self-expression and individuality. There are no knots with this center.

Exercise

You can balance Manipura by using the pit pose.

1. Lie on your belly, with your hands on top of each other, beneath your solar plexus, just a few inches above the navel. You may fold your hands into fists if it's comfortable.

2. Take long, deep breaths while you press both hands into the navel, massaging your stomach muscles with just your breath moving against your hands.

3. When a minute has passed, pull your hands out from beneath you and relax.

Psychic Abilities

When you master this chakra, you have freedom from sickness. You are set free from fire, which means it can't harm you even if you're in a furnace. However, please don't throw yourself into one to test this!

Manipura mastery means you can live a life longer than most, finding the cure for diseases, and growing in your understanding of how the body works. You demonstrate this chakra's creative and destructive power and can create your own gold and find all hidden treasure. With it, you become claircognizant. You develop mental empathy, and the gift of pyrokinesis, which allows you to start fires with just your mind.

Auric Layer

The third auric layer is just on top of the second one, about ten inches away from your skin.

Secondary Chakras

Your Manipura has two major secondary energy centers: the surya or hrit chakra and the manas or mind chakra. The surya gives Manipura the heat element, which is why Tibetan Buddhists call it the fire wheel. The manas are between the navel and heart and sometimes just above the third eye or brow chakra. When it's in your lower body, it is connected to the five senses and your mind. According to Tibetan Buddhists, it's shown with six spokes when it's on your forehead (also called the wind wheel).

Chapter Six: The Heart Chakra - Anahata

The heart chakra allows you to make decisions that have nothing to do with your karma's restrictions. It helps you to stay on the path that feels the most authentic to you, regardless of material temptations that could sway you off course. Within this center, you deal with all of life's shadows, including anxiety, defiance, and lust, so it allows you to keep your honor and remain compassionate so you can be your best self. When your Anahata wakes up, you can overcome all violence since everything you're about is deeply rooted in love.

The Anahata's Qualities

Anahata is Sanskrit for "unbeaten or unhurt." It also means "unstruck sound." When all vital breath or prana flows through your Sushumna into the maniura, the seed sounds will show up in your fourth chakra. These sounds depend on the width and shape of the nadis. The more air pressure there is on Anahata, the more pronounced the seed sound would naturally be. It's called the unstruck sound because all the sounds of the letters that show up are pronounced with no friction.

The Anahata lies between your breasts, in the same area as the heart. It aligns with the Sushumna nadi, which is its sound's source. It splits the body into two hemispheres—upper and lower. The lower hemisphere represents consciousness in its primitive forms, where all that concerns you is physical pleasures. The higher hemisphere comprises the higher chakras, which connect with consciousness in spiritual form.

Anahata becomes active from the ages of twenty-one to twenty-eight, according to the Hindu chakra system. This is when we become very aware of the consequences of our choices and actions, which create our karma. It's the point when you've got to decide to act from a place of devotion and love so that you can be a balanced person.

Body Parts

There are two organs connected to Anahata: the heart, which is also an endocrine gland, and the thymus gland. Anahata handles the heart, blood, circulatory system, breasts, rib cage, lungs, hands, arms, and shoulders. Along with other energy centers, it also manages the esophagus and the diaphragm.

Some insist that the heart isn't an endocrine gland, while others say it is. It's a muscle about the size of your fist, responsible for pumping blood nonstop all through your body. The heart has two ventricles at the bottom and two atria at the top. Coronary arteries on its surface feed it, giving it blood rich in oxygen. Valves connect the heart's chambers, and it has nerve tissues that send complex signals to and from the brain to keep the heart pumping.

The heart is an endocrine gland that secretes quite the array of neurotransmitters and hormones like the love bonding oxytocin, which your brain also secretes. Because of how unique the heart is, you could say it works almost like a brain. It sends out signals through your vagus nerve and spinal column to your actual brain to dictate what should happen with the endocrine and nervous systems, the urinary and digestive tracts, the lymph and respiratory systems, the spleen, and various brain functions.

When you experience positive emotions, your brain will create a healthy balance in your body. You will also find that you're able to earn more money, and your relationships become even better than ever. On the flip side, feeling terrible — when dealing with anger and fear, for instance — will have an adverse effect on every aspect of your life.

Exercise

You must keep your heart safe from fear. It responds to it easily. You know this when you feel your heart skip a beat or beat faster or slower as you give in to negative, fearful thoughts. Often, we spend a lot of time regretting past mistakes and worrying about future outcomes. So, the following mantra will help you let go of all fear and fill your heart with peace. Here's what you need to do:

1. Find a comfy spot to sit in. Make sure it's quiet and that you won't be disturbed or distracted.

2. Shut your eyes and chant this mantra: om shante sarvarishta nashini swaha. What this means is "Sacred one, towards peace. You are the way to attain freedom from all suffering. This is my prayer."

3. Repeat this mantra repeatedly, either aloud or silently, while breathing in a relaxed manner. Feel yourself being cleansed of all fears and worries. Release them with trust to the Divine.

Major Sense

The Anahata's main sense is touch, and the skin is the primary organ.

Action Organ

The sexual organ is the action organ.

Vital Breath

Prana is the vital breath.

Related Illnesses

When the Anahata is in trouble, one can face diseases that affect the breasts, lungs, heart, ribs, and pericardium. Asthma, heart diseases, pneumonia, cancer, thoracic spinal issues, thymus problems, shoulder and upper back issues are also the result of trouble with the Anahata.

Psychology

The heart is where all positive emotion is felt. It is the seat of love. It governs all relationships, including your relationship with yourself, other people around you, and the Source. This energy center shows you how to balance your emotional needs in relationships with others so you can be generous while also taking care of yourself. It shows you how to keep from losing yourself while loving another.

Anahata helps you break free of karma's bonds, so the decisions you make are honorable and transcend your past. Learn to follow your heart. In simple English, this means you need to learn to see things from a higher lane and decide from a place of generosity and thoughtfulness, instead of just giving in to your compulsions and desires.

Archetypes

The Anahata's positive archetype is the Lover, which oversees feeling, emotion, sensuality, and idealism. It takes life's mysterious forces and fills it with joy each day. The negative archetype is the Actor. The Actor loves to make exaggerations in their life. They'll lie and do anything they can to get attention, especially by using traumatic experiences. This archetype can teach you to take your passion for telling false stories and use that instead for sharing insight and wisdom by crafting inspirational stories, legends, and myths instead.

Personality

The one who lives from the heart is drawn to people in love. They can easily tell what works for them and what doesn't. If you are this person, then happiness and love matter the most to you. You also tend to fix other couples' problems. You love to serve others, particularly by acting as a healing force.

Excesses and Deficiencies

When Anahata is deficient, you cannot forgive, you lack self-love and empathy, you're lonely, indifferent, apathetic, withdrawn, and feel purposeless. When there are excesses, you become codependent and jealous. Self-centeredness, martyrdom, tribalism, self-aggrandizement, and egotism become the order of the day.

Balanced Anahata

When there's balance in this center, you feel whole. You also are very nurturing, accepting, compassionate, empathetic, motivating, and friendly.

Anahata Yantra

The symbol is a lotus flower, smokey-gray, with twelve petals. It has a shaktona, which signifies the feminine and masculine union, as seen from the triangles, which overlap and intersect to create a hexagram. The upward-facing triangle is a symbol of Shiva, while the downward-facing triangle is Shakti. The hexagram is a symbol of the Supreme Being or Purusha, and the mother of matter, Prakriti. Vayu is the deity of this region, also colored like smoke, and with four arms. Vayu holds a goading stick and proudly rides the antelope, which is the Anahata's sound carrier.

In Anahata, you'll find the dark gray seed syllable yam. In the dot that is above the syllable is Ishana, a deity we'll discuss soon enough. You can also find the Kakini, which is the Shakti form connected with Ishana.

Parts of the Anahata

The gross element is air, while the subtle element is touch or impact. The element's color is tepid green, gray, and is sometimes colorless. Its sound is yam. This center's attributes are restlessness and patience. The sound carrier is the gazelle or the black antelope, both of which serve as symbols of lightness in physical matter. That they're both swifts also represents the air element and Purusha. The shy, graceful antelope is also a sign that nothing about spirit can be grasped, measured, or appreciated by anyone who lives from his or her ego. The Anahata has twelve petals, all vermillion in color. They are all symbols for the vrittis of incompetence, arrogance, fraud, lust, anxiety, repentance, hope, longing, indecision, defiance, discrimination, impartiality, and arrogance. Vrittis are thoughts that go through the mind, affecting us positively or negatively.

Cosmic Plane

He Anahata is connected to the home of saints and siddhis, the mahar loka realm, where balance reigns supreme.

Gods and Goddesses

Kakini Shakti rules, with her sky-blue sari and rosy skin, as she sits on a pink lotus, holding a trident, skill, shield, and sword. Also ruling is Ishana Rudra Shiva, or Isvara, a benevolent and peaceful god with skin blue like camphor. He has a drum in his left hand and a trident in his right one. His hair flows, a symbol of the Ganges, and a representation of the knowledge of self in which one declares "I Am That." There are snakes wrapped around his body, signifying that he has tamed his passions. The ruling planet is Venus, which has the energies of beauty, love, and pleasure.

Granthi or Knot

The second Kundalini lock is the Vishnu granthi, which is connected to the body's abdominal valve and Anahata. Some say it lies between Anahata and Manipura. Vishnu, being the god of preservation, calls unto us to undo this knot so we can become more compassionate. This means we choose to accept that it's okay to serve others with loving devotion and let go of self and ego.

Psychic Abilities

When you have control of the air element, you will gain your Anahata siddhi or abilities. Among them are bhuchari siddhi, which lets you travel wherever you want, khechari siddhi, which allows you to fly through the sky, and kaya siddhi, which sets you free from old age, illness, and death.

You also gain in-depth knowledge of the present, past, and future, and clairvoyance and clairaudience. You can also find the cure for all manners of sicknesses, get insight into physiology, create and destroy energies, create gold, and discover all hidden treasures. You also gain gifts like the ability to hear from a great distance, change your physical form, enter another person's body (whether they're alive or dead), die when you want to, lay with the heavenly gods in their sports, and have every one of your commands fulfilled.

You also gain the gifts of apantomancy (the ability to gain meaning from "accidental" meetings with various creatures), astral projection, palmistry or chiromancy, energetic healing, hypnosis, faith healing, clairempathy (sensing other people's emotions), and megagnomy (using your psychic powers while in a trance).

Auric Layer

The fourth auric layer is above the third, a foot and a half away from your skin.

Secondary Chakra

The hrit chakra lies beneath the heart, close to the solar plexus, at the left of your body. This is your spiritual heart, with the anandakanda, which is its own lotus. Anandakanda means "bulb or root of bliss," and it has eight petals which correspond to anger, joy, evil, dullness, holiness, charity, and sexuality. The petals are red, gold, or white.

Hrit is Sanskrit for the heart. It is found in the vertebral column and is shown as a subtle energy center that is stain-free, as nothing impure can touch it. It faces downwards, making up Anahata's lower region.

This secondary center is also called hridaya chakra, which means "He who dwells in the heart," or the anandakanda chakra, which is where matter and energy unite to create bliss. It's golden and is called the sun chakra or surya, with connections to the Manipura because it gives heat to the third primary energy center.

The hrit has three regions. The first is a sun, vermillion in color, encompassing a white moon. In the moon is a region deep red, and within that is the enchanted kalpataru, a tree that grants wishes, allowing the manifestation of your deepest desires. This celestial wishing tree has an altar decked with jewels before it. It was the tree given to all of mankind from Indra's Heaven, red, just like a new dawn. It is often said that you get even more than what you wish for with this tree.

According to Tibetan Buddhism, Anahata is connected to the white and red drop, also called the "fire wheel." This wheel is what transports your consciousness to your next life, serving as its very own chakra. It is white, circular, and has eight petals that point downwards. The seed syllable is hum. Tantric Tibetan culture says this chakra sits between the throat and heart chakras.

Exercise: To Wish Upon a Celestial Tree

This tree will grant you the most earnest of your wishes. It's not about having a million dollars or a lover in your bed. It will grant you whatever your soul desires the most. You need only to be sincere in your asking, and you will get even more than you request. This tree will give you freedom. You're about to carry out meditation to allow you to connect with the tree. Here's how to proceed:

1. Lie in a comfy position.

2. Take long, deep, relaxing breaths.

3. As you breathe, notice your heartbeat.

4. Follow your blood as it pumps throughout your body, moving through arteries, veins, and capillaries. Feel how it's just like a tree. Imagine your legs are roots connecting you to the Earth.

5. Turn your focus or awareness of the tree close to your heart chakra. This is just beneath the ribs and to your left. Indra planted this tree, the kalpataru, in your hrit chakra.

6. Visualize the altar with jewels inlaid in it, right before the tree. In your mind's eye, kneel at the altar.

7. Commit to live a life of service, devoted to the highest good. This is essential to allow your heart chakra to work as it should, accessing the blessings of kalpataru.

8. Take your time to focus on what your soul desires. Think about what feels true to you and what desires that you deeply seek to see come to fruition.

9. Allow yourself to feel the hunger you have for these desires. Let them take over your body. Feel them pulsing through you, much like the blood flows through you.

10. Allow the pulsation to move to your kalpataru, directing and channeling all desires by simply shifting your attention to its location.

11. Imagine your desires are like rainfall, completely drenching the kalpataru.

12. See a bird fly in from a distance and then perch on the tree. Watch it cock its head as it listens to your desires and hopes, absorbing them all.

13. When the bird has sensed that you are ready to let go of your desires and allow the Divine to sort out how to deliver them to you, feel the bird gently kissing you with its beak, and then watch it fly off into the distance, carrying your hopes and dreams off to Indra, who will be grand all you have requested.

14. Once the bird is no longer in sight, feel your heart fill with gratitude for the gift of the kalpataru, which is always within you, waiting for you to make your wishes known.

15. Give gratitude to the bird and Indra as well, for the wonderful ways you will receive your desires.

16. Take a few long, satisfying breaths, and then come back out of your meditation. You may now wait for your manifestations, keeping your heart open to all that comes your way.

Chapter Seven: The Throat Chakra - Vishuddha

According to Indian mythology, devas and rakshasas (gods and demons) have always battled it out with one another. During one battle, Vishnu intended to end it all by causing the ocean to churn and roll, much as the mind does. As the waters swirled, two things came out of the deep—the nectar that gives immortality and poison.

The gods took the nectar, but no one would have the poison. As such, Shiva drank it so he could get rid of the danger. The venom remained in his throat. This is why Shiva is called Nilakantha, which means "the blue-throated one." Because of his selflessness, when we learn of the Vishuddha chakra and choose to work with it actively, we can use its power to get rid of all of life's toxic elements. Words can transform your life for better or worse. That is why the ancient, wise saying goes, "Death and life are in the power of the tongue."

The nectar from the churning ocean is called amrita. It drips from your bindu chakra, which sits in your head's fontanel area, showing you how to be more expressive of your true self, give in to creativity, and exercise more positive discrimination in your daily affairs. This allows your terrible experiences to change or be transmuted into much-needed wisdom. In the process, all blocks are eradicated — particularly the very significant block of guilt. You communicate with sound, and from a much higher place, you can listen to everything going on around you. With time, you too can become the epitome of Vishuddha, which is total communication.

Vishuddha is Sanskrit for "purification." You can find it right in line with the nadi of the Sushumna, at the bottom of the throat. It is connected to the carotid plexus and the laryngeal plexus, too. The middle of the throat is where it activates. The activation point is called the kshetram. This center is the foundation of expression and communication. It's sky blue, and sometimes a bright turquoise as well. According to the Hindu chakra system, this center becomes active between ages 28 and 35. This is when it becomes vital to us to express our knowledge of the divine and wisdom that is uncommon and useful to all.

Body Parts

This fifth energy center has the thyroid as its gland. This gland is shaped like a butterfly and sits right beneath the Adam's apple, just along the trachea's anterior region. It has two lobes at the side, which connect in the middle.

The thyroid has a lot of nerves and blood vessels and is important for secreting necessary hormones in the body, and the chief among them is thyroxine or T4. T4 works with other thyroid hormones to deal with your growth, metabolism, body temperature, and development. Among the various thyroid issues are hyper- and hypothyroidism, exhaustion, Graves' disease, and digestive issues. How healthy this organ depends on how you're able to express yourself with your Vishuddha. It also depends on how you're able to keep a lid on the ability of external entities to access the entry point of this energy center, which allows you to receive celestial guidance.

Each dysfunction that affects the thyroid has a unique meaning from an energy point of view. There are many instances where their healthcare professional tells women that their thyroid is normal, yet they have a lot of symptoms that could only be connected to a thyroid problem. This happens because the test conducted is only for T4, rather than the efficient conversion of that hormone to T3. As a matter of fact, T4 is the hormone derived from the conversion of iodine. T3 or triiodothyronine is also synthesized from iodine. The cells in this organ work to combine amino acid tyrosine and iodine to create both hormones, with T3 being the more active one and T4 broken down further.

When the body can't convert T4 to T3, then the metabolic rate suffers and slows down. This happens because of a lack of the essential minerals needed, like calcium, magnesium, and iodine, among others. It could also be caused by excess stress, especially in people who are too busy taking care of everyone else but themselves.

Major Sense

Hearing is the major sense of this chakra, and the sense organs are the ears.

Action Organ

The mouth is the action organ.

Vital Breath

The udana is this center's vital breath.

Related Illnesses

Bronchitis, asthma, thyroid infections, laryngitis, sore throat, mouth ulcers, hearing issues, ear infections, gum and teeth issues, mouth issues, neck issues, tonsillitis, tinnitus, hay fever, upper arm pain, laryngitis, and temporomandibular joint dysfunctions are some of the health issues connected with this energy center.

Psychology

This center governs matters of faith, personal expression, decision-making, and creativity. It's also what helps us determine what we should voice and what we shouldn't. It helps you figure out how to say whatever you decide to say. Mastering this center is vital because it would allow you to communicate from an authentic place with honesty rooted in kindness. When you choose falsehood and lies, the chakra becomes polluted. You stay silent, act evasive, and repress your anger — none of which are good for you.

Your Vishuddha is particularly affected by beliefs you could never attain your desires or that you should never stand up and speak up on your own behalf. When you don't know who you are, you tend to give in to vices like gossiping and lying. Your emotions feel like they've got a chokehold on you (sometimes literally!), and you can't help but criticize yourself and others at every turn. The main obstacle you need to overcome is to face your past karma and behavior. You also need to be willing to let go of all guilt. Set yourself free and grant yourself forgiveness because you deserve it and because it's the only way you can move forward in life.

Archetypes

The positive archetype of this center is the Communicator, who, according to Jung, uses all the means of communication to gather information and disperse it accordingly. The negative archetype is the Silent Child, who refuses to communicate truthfully, and would rather suppress and stifle their needs and emotions. The Silent Child can be transmuted to good when you learn the difference between when you should say something or nothing.

Personality

The person who has an active fifth chakra is about communication. They love anything that gets the point across, whether it's words or music – if the message is sent and received by all relevant parties. If this is you, you'll find you have strong opinions and no issues expressing them. You're also a great listener, and you tend to pick up on things faster by saying them aloud. Spiritually, you are destined to communicate either through speech or music, sending along with your spiritual messages to all who need them.

Many who have a strong fifth chakra will wind up being excellent communicators and make good money from this gift. You could also be an introvert and an excellent communicator as well so don't feel like you need to count yourself out with this gift. If you're particularly gifted, no matter how shy you are, you will find you can speak up, and when you do, you can access your Vishuddha's backside, which grants you divine guidance in what to say and how to say it.

Excesses and Deficiencies

When there are deficiencies in this chakra, it leads to teeth grinding, an underactive thyroid, a fear of speaking, throat illnesses, and the inability to speak your truth. You might also find that you're a tad too precise about how you use words.

When your chakra suffers excessively, you might find yourself dealing with stuttering, gossiping, loudness, an inability to be considerate, fragmentation, and an overactive thyroid. The excesses can also lead you to compulsive actions like overeating.

Balanced Vishuddha

When your fifth chakra is balanced, you are very expressive and creative. You communicate in an uplifting, positive way. You listen consciously, intending to understand and make others feel heard. You feel content in general.

Vishuddha Yantra

This chakra's yantra is a silver crescent that lies in a white circle reminiscent of the moon at its fullest. Many people see the crescent as being on the bottom or "tail" of the symbol in the middle.

The white moon is in a sky-blue triangle that points downwards. Around this triangle are sixteen petals. The silver crescent symbolizes the nada's lunar symbol, a cosmic sound that is pure. It represents the required purification you must have when energy has ascended to this energy center.

In the white portion of this chakra is the elephant, which is its sound carrier. It is represented on top of this elephant. Ambhara is the god in charge of bija ham. All white, he sits on his elephant, with four arms. He holds a goad and a noose, and he grants blessings and removes all fear. In his laps, you will also find deities, gods, and goddesses we shall cover shortly.

In this chakra, you can see the amrita nectar dripping through the chitrini nadi, divided into its pure form and its poisonous form. The moon's image is a symbol of clairvoyance, psychic energy, and the ability to communicate with no words. When these abilities become active, helped by the inner Shakti, who gives all siddhis or abilities, all the lower chakra's elements (Earth, fire, water, and air) become refined and will dissolve into akasha or ether.

Parts of Vishuddha

The gross element of this center is akasha, also called ether. This is the combination of the essence of the five classical elements, but it has no touch, color, smell, taste, or form of its own. The subtle element is sound or vibration, and its color is a smoky purple. The element's sound is ham, and ego and unity are its attributes.

Airavata is the elephant sound carrier and the master of all herbivores. He is also the vehicle Indra uses for transportation. Sometimes he's depicted as white or a smoky gray, just like the clouds, and represents purity. Airavata has no restrictions and can move as he pleases in etheric planes, remaining open to the cosmos' rays. His trunk creates the ng sound, which is a pure, powerful nasal sound that transports energy to the outer cortex of your brain, and this is where your impressions of life are stored. This sound allows you to turn those impressions into valuable wisdom and knowledge so you are set free from the cycle of reincarnation.

There are sixteen petals on this chakra, colored smoky purple or smoke, and possessing one letter each, being golden, red, or deep red. From right to left, they are:

- Am
- Aam
- Im
- Iim
- Um
- Uum
- Rm
- Rrm
- Lm
- Llm
- Em
- Alm
- Om
- Aum
- Aam
- Ahm

The bija mantra of the fifth energy center is ham, which is pronounced like the word "hang." You'll need to shape your lips like an oval and push the air out from your throat as you keep your focus on the lower neck's curve.

Cosmic Plane

The jana loka is the Vishuddha's plane. It is the ending of darkness.

Gods and Goddesses

Shakini has five faces, four arms, and three eyes. She's usually shown as being a shining yellow or white. She typically holds a goad, noose, trident, and bow and arrow. Sitting on a red lotus, Shakini gives you higher divine knowledge. She gives you mastery of psychic communication and the five elements.

Then there's Sadashiva in the form of Ardhanarishvara. The right of his body is the Shiva part, often white. The left side is the Shakti side, and it's golden. Being androgynous, Ardhanarishvara teaches us to unite our feminine and masculine aspects beautifully. He has ten arms, five faces, and three eyes. He holds a chisel or an ax, a trident, a fire, a thunderbolt or vajra, a bell, a goad, a snake, and a noose. He also makes a gesture that banishes all fear.

Another god — an alternative - is Panchavaktra Shiva, whose skin is camphor blue. He has five heads, which represent the five senses, and the five lower chakras in a state of perfection. His face represents Shiva's five aspects, Ishana, Aghora, Mahadeva, Rudra, and Sadashiva. This god will always manifest the aum sound. The ruling planet of Vishuddha is mercury, which is the planet of learning and all mental activity. There are no granthis or knots with this center.

Exercise

The khechari mudra will open the energy body to receive the nectar that flows down into Vishuddha. It also allows a connection with the chakra found in your mouth's soft palate. This mudra is also called the tongue-lock or tongue-swallowing technique, as you have to turn your tongue up and then slide it back into the nasal cavity right above your soft palate.

There are so many reasons you should perform this mudra. For starters, it will stimulate some pressure points which lie behind the mouth, within the nasal cavity, and this will then activate a bunch of glands to increase saliva and the secretion of helpful, necessary hormones. It works to reduce your thirst and hunger and can cause you to feel calmer and more serene. This technique moves the nectar from the back area of the fontanel and downwards.

When you do this technique, there will be pressure in the throat area and both of your carotid sinuses, which sit at the sides of the main artery that supplies blood to your brain. They sit beneath your jaw, at the front of your neck, regulating your blood pressure and flow. When they notice that your blood pressure is falling, they tell your brain to increase your heartbeat and contract particular blood vessels until your blood pressure stabilizes. When the blood pressure is high, they tell your brain to do the opposite. When you work with this area energetically, you will feel less stressed and more alive. Here's how to practice this mudra:

1. Roll your tongue up and backward. You want its lower part to touch your upper palate. Stretch as far as you can to the back, but don't strain your tongue.

2. Inhale, and as you do, create a snoring sound using the back of your throat. Then breathe out.

3. If saliva forms, you can swallow it, so you don't feel uncomfortable. If you find that you're too uncomfortable, it's okay to release your tongue, rest it for a bit and then put it back in the lock.

4. Continue with this practice daily until you're able to sustain the lock for five to ten minutes each session while breathing in and out just five or six times a minute. If you notice that there's a bitter taste as you do this, then stop the practice immediately because it means you are secreting poisons. You can try again later.

Psychic Abilities

Mastering the qualities of this chakra is known as the akashi-dharana. When you hit this level, you will never perish, even if all of life does. You gain knowledge about the present, past, and future. You also gain freedom from thirst and hunger, clairaudience, the ability to levitate, super hearing, teleportation, and mastery of your five senses and the five elements. You grow in knowledge. Your eloquence also grows, and you have no trouble persuading people, even putting them under your spell through hypnosis.

Other gifts you may have are the ability to communicate with the dead, bibliomancy (interpreting the real meaning of book passages), automatic writing (delivering messages from a divine source in a trance state in written form), channeling (the same as automatic writing, but in spoken words), and exorcism (setting people free from spirits). You may also have clairaudience, megagnomy, telepathy, xenoglossy (speaking a language you don't understand or know), mediumship (serving as a channel for a spirit to speak through), hypnosis, transfiguration (putting on another face), and clairgustance.

Auric Layer

The fifth auric layer is above the fourth, two feet away from your skin. There are "Secret chakras" connected to higher ones, and several of them connect to the Vishuddha. Lalana is one at the bottom of the nasal orifice, right above your throat. The bindu visarga is on top of your brain, at the back of your head. It's where Hindu monks will leave a bit of hair. Along with the Vishuddha, a triangle is formed.

Sahasrara gives the nectar, which is collected in the bindu visarga. It translates to "falling of drops." This nectar is so potent that yogis have survived on it when buried for forty days straight. When the Vishuddha is not active, the nectar heads down to Manipura, where you begin to degenerate.

Lalana means "tongue" and "female energy." It sits at the base of your palate, at the back of your uvula. To meditate on this, you need a guru's guidance. A lot of tantric texts say Kundalini passes on to Ajna through lalana.

The Saubhagya Lakshmi Upanishad says that the lalana has 12 petals, all bright red. Other texts claim it has 64 petals, silvery-white, which is the ghantika, a pericarp that's bright red. In that pericarp is where the nectar flows from, known as the chandra kala, or moon energy.

The 64 petals contain 64 great yoginis who can teach you, and as you practice with them, you can unlock eight special siddhis. Lalana is connected with 12 nadis that allow you to gain all knowledge. It's also called talana and is sometimes stated as being above the Ajna when it's not the lalata instead (another secret chakra). The golata chakra is beneath the lalana, just on the uvula. Together, all these chakras are called the Mouth of God.

Your Vishuddha pulses with akasha's element, which shows up as sound or vibration, is a smoky purple and has the unity element. It allows you to communicate and respond to other people as they communicate in such a way there is unity between us all.

Chapter Eight: The Third Eye Chakra - Ajna

The third eye chakra is connected to the mind. It has to do with physical, psychic, and inner vision. This allows you to move beyond your individual consciousness and rise above duality.

Think of this as the "chakra of threes." There are the lunar and solar nadis, the Ida, and the Pingala, which connect with the Sushumna or central channel, moving towards a transcendent level of consciousness. There are the three gunas — rajas, sattva, and tamas — which connect to create the aum, which is the divine and most sacred sound. In the fires of Ajna are the elements of consciousness, also three in number:

- Buddhi (higher mind)
- Ahamkara (ego)
- Manas (thinking mind)

The Ajna's Qualities

Ajna is Sanskrit for "summoning, authority, unlimited power, and command." This center directs all energetic affairs of the others. Ajna is also called bhrumadhya. Bhru means "eyebrows," and madhya means "in-between." This is the location of Ajna. It's called trikuti, which means "third eye," and is an acknowledgment of the clairvoyant power it bestows on the one who has worked with it actively. You may also hear it called the forehead, sixth, brow, or third eye chakra.

The Ajna is right at the top of your spinal column. It sits in the medulla oblongata, which is the lower portion of your brain stem. It is also connected to your medulla or cavernous plexus. However, it's not so easy to spot its precise location, so many people put their attention on its activation point, which is in the middle of your eyebrows. The Ajna allows you to have perception and vision. It's indigo or violet in color. According to the Hindu chakra system, there isn't a set time when this one becomes active. But, if there had to be one, it would be between ages 35 and 42.

Body Parts

The Ajna is connected to the pituitary and the pineal glands. The pituitary gland is a little endocrine organ. It's pea-sized and is right in the center of the brain. It sits in a cavity of round bone kept apart from your sphenoid sinus by another thin bone that acts as the sinus' roof region, the part that's right at the back. Your sphenoid's drainage moves down to the part of your nasal cavity's opening. This explains why, according to Hindu belief, there is nectar that drops down from above into the Ajna. The sphenoid sinus is found adjacent to your optic nerve, which allows you to see. Your pituitary gland is connected to this nerve — as is the pineal gland, allowing you to activate your Ajna abilities.

The pituitary oversees creating hormones that regulate sex, growth, kidneys, muscles and other endocrine glands in your body. It is the storehouse for all the hypothalamus' hormones. It's the master gland that controls several organs and glands, including the gonads, thyroid, and adrenals. It has two lobes. The anterior one handles reproduction growth and metabolism, and that's about 80 percent of the pituitary's purpose. The posterior lobe creates oxytocin and vasopressin, both of which are connected to Kundalini. It releases these hormones when the pituitary receives messages from the hypothalamus through nerve cells.

There's a stalk-like structure connecting the pituitary and hypothalamus, which shows the connection between them. The latter handles several bodily processes, like hunger, temperature regulation, thirst, circadian rhythms, attachment, sleep, and parenting. Biologically speaking, the pituitary's posterior region is the hypothalamus' extension, while the anterior region is independent. The nerves that handle this relationship between the pituitary and hypothalamus are also in charge of sexual activity and emotions.

The hypothalamus also actively regulates the aging process, slowing it down or speeding it up. It does this in response to inflammation in the body — or even by creating inflammation. Inflammation causes pain and is the reason for health issues like diabetes, heart diseases, and gene degeneration, which leads to more aging and troubling illnesses.

The third eye is associated with the lizard's parietal eye. Granted, it's not as functional as the human eyes, but it does respond to light. This parietal eye used to be in crocodiles, turtles, and birds, but evolution has done away with it in these creatures. It is a lined structure that supports the brain's two symmetrical parts. With time, the right part becomes a pineal sac that releases melatonin, while the left becomes the parietal eye, which takes in light. This regulates the sleep cycle. As a human, you have a pineal gland, not a sac.

The pituitary gland's structure is vital for how you view yourself and your ability to manifest your desires, and how these two factors are connected. The front part of the pituitary gland is responsible for taking in your life choices, all of which come in through the Ajna's posterior region. This region sends forth your decisions, which then become the path that takes you to the future you desire.

The space that lies empty in the middle is where you hold your perceptions of yourself. You choose the future you desire from the choices you get based on what you think about yourself. Enlightenment is not just about your perception of the nature of Spirit, but your acceptance of the way Spirit sees you.

The Ajna manages the pituitary gland, sinuses, eyes, brain, pineal gland, hypothalamus, parts of the ears, and the nose. It doesn't have a major sense, as it is a neutral center. However, the mind is its sense organ (perceiving things with the five senses and more) and its action organ. Ajna also has no vital breath of its own, working instead with every vital breath in a harmonic balance.

Related Illnesses

Illnesses connected to this chakra include nightmares, deafness, eyesight issues, brain tumors, blindness, seizures, depression, strokes, insomnia, acute sinusitis, nervous breakdowns, blood pressure issues, dyslexia, pain, hormone imbalances, dizziness, neuralgia, developmental and growth disorders, learning disabilities, and along with other energy centers, migraines.

Psychology

When your third eye chakra is developed, you become a seer. You gain a deep understanding of the truth—we are all of one spirit though we are many. All separation is merely an illusion and nothing more. Do not mistake this to be a state in which you're perpetually blissful. Instead, this is a state in which you may live life simply, thanks to this awareness. You can do this because you now have mastery over your mental, cognitive, and intellectual abilities.

If you have any issues with this center, you have to deal with things like being intensely irritated with someone else or some part of your life. It will be hard to perceive the truth about what's going on around you at the moment. If you know someone who isn't willing to change their old ways and patterns, even though they do not serve them and give unpleasant results, then they have issues with this chakra to work out. The same goes for those who cannot think optimistically of the future or find something joyful to look forward to.

The Ajna issues you could face are a matter of perception. Be deliberate about seeing the good in all. You want to look at life through the eyes of the Divine, through your higher consciousness, not the lies you've been programmed to believe about how you could never be enough. Accept that you're more than enough. You are worthy of being here now. Your worth is not dependent on your skills or what you can or cannot do. That you exist right now is all the proof you need to realize that you matter. You're reading this because the Divine, Source, Infinite Intelligence, God, your Higher Self, or whatever you call the sum of all your parts that you can't perceive with your five senses, thought you were worthy enough to breathe, live, and be. Accept this, and you will find the "peace that surpasses all understanding."

Archetypes

The positive archetype of this energy center is Intuitive, which is the opposite of the Sensor. While the latter gets information through the physical senses, the former can perceive reality by channels more subtle and far beyond just the five senses. The Intuitive can perceive future possibilities and knows the unconscious energy that permeates the "here" in any given "now."

The negative archetype is the Intellectual, who is unfeeling, cold, and manipulative. The Intellectual solves problems and is very analytical. They cannot trust or understand matters of the spirit. Though, the Intellectual can remain detached and logical, which allows them to further explore the truth about the infinite because they are. They don't become so overwhelmed that they lose their grounding and ignore real and present physical needs.

Personality

The person with this chakra is an expert at long-term planning and is drawn to the future. If this is you, you see the big picture. You play a long game. You're a very visual person, and that's how you process information, too, because thought, emotions, and words are all translated to their picture equivalent in your mind. You have a spiritual purpose that needs you to see a positive future for one and all and use your vision to help guide everyone to a wonderful end.

Excesses and Deficiencies

When you're deficient in energy within this center, you can't see what's right in front of you. You deny the challenges or problems you have and leave yourself open to being deceived. You experience codependency, chaos, trouble with planning for the future, abusive relationships, a lack of joy, memory loss, anxiety, and perception problems.

When the Ajna suffers excesses, the result is that you can't concentrate, you fantasize a lot, suffer hallucinations, nightmares, delusions, obsessiveness, turmoil, and self-centeredness.

Balanced Ajna

When your Ajna is balanced, you have a strong intuition, a keen intellect, and the ability to imagine positively. You see the larger picture, perceive spiritual planes (and even influence them), set goals, and instantly act on them to get the needed results.

Ajna Yantra

This center is depicted by a triangle pointing downwards or a trikona, known as the tritasra. The triangle sits in a circle, with two petals extending from the circle to create a lotus. The corners of the triangle are connected with Vishnu, Brahma, and Maheshvara, who is a Shiva form that destroys and restores worlds.

Within the yona is the Shiva form known as Itara, in the Shiva lingam or phallic form. The lingam is either shining white, golden, or red and is reminiscent of lightning streaks. It is a bindu point in the triangle's center and a sign of the causal world, with connections to the Rudra knot.

The lotus' seed vessel is apericarp, which has vital seeds. In energy centers, it contains a lot of symbols and images. Within Ajna, Shakti Hakini is enclosed by the pericarp, with the moon white lingam above her. Some chakra systems have Ardhanarishvara, which is Shiva's and Shakti's hermaphrodite form, within the lingam. There are other systems where you first see Hakinin within the pericarp, with the itara linga just above her, and aum (the seed syllable or pranava) within the triangle that hangs above him, and the manas symbol (mind tattva) on top. The Ajna has two white petals.

The amrita or soma nectar sits in the Ajna kshetram's hollow, where the Sushumna, ida, and Pingala meet in an area called trikuti or triatha sthana, in the space between your brows. This is a red hexagon. Because of the junction, the heagonal area is called muktha triveni, meaning "three strands creating liberty."

Parts of the Ajna

The gross element is light, while the subtle element is the supreme element, encompassing all other elements. It is transparent in color, and the sound is Om. Its attributes are ego and unity. While the center isn't always tied to a sound carrier, it's often connected to the black antelope when it is.

The Ajna's lotus is a beautiful and radiant white like the moon. Its two petals have ha (or ham) and ksa (or ksham) inscribed on them in white, too. The petals represent the nadis of the ida and Pingala — the moon and sun energy — both connect in the central channel of the Sushumna before moving up to the crown chakra. The left petal symbolizes Shiva, while the right petal represents Shakti. These are the mind, manifested and unmanifested, respectively. The petals are dynamic, radiating power. One sends the energy flowing down to the five lower chakras, while the other sends energy to the higher ones. Within this radiation of power are the five divine powers, the five vayus, and Kundalini. The lotus is luminescent with the dhyana's glory or the act of meditation.

Cosmic Plane

The cosmic plane is the home of the blessed and the realm of austerity known as the tapas loka.

Gods and Goddesses

Hakini is white and holds a white moon, book, skull, rosary, and a mudra that grants favors and banishes fear. She has six faces, red in color, with three eyes in each one. Her throne is the white lotus.

Shiva is the god of the divine dance and destruction. He has mastery over all his desires, which he gained through the act of meditation. This chakra is also connected to Ardhanarishvara, the blend of the masculine and feminine Shiva and Shakti. This androgynous god has the white Shiva on the right and the golden Shakti on the left. Ajna is the point of clairvoyance, and Shiva's third eye is called sva-netra, which is the organ of clairvoyance. This center's ruling planet is the watery Neptune, which is all about psychic activity and mystery.

Granthi

The Ajna is connected to the third Kundalini knot or granthi, called the Rudra knot. It is connected with the itara linga, which shines with white lightning. This is the causal world's symbol and the state of androgyny. Rudra is Shiva, the god of destruction. This granthi seeks to help you see all things as holy and sacred. When you untie this knot, your Kundalini can rise to this energy center, and your consciousness will move on up to the Sahasrara, and then dimensions further than that.

Psychic Abilities

As you work with Ajna, you destroy your past life karma and receive all the eight major siddhis, and the 32 minor siddhis. Before you can attain all these siddhis, though, you must be detached from them and not consider them so special. If you do not, you will always remain connected to the three gunas, unable to live life as a being aware of their nonduality.

Mastery of Ajna brings aeromancy (divination using the clouds and weather), alomancy (divination by reading the pattern of thrown salt), catoptromancy (divination with mirrors), aura reading, cleromancy (divination by casting stones or bones), clairvoyance, crystallomancy (divination using crystal balls), gyromancy (deviation by drawing a circle, marking its perimeter with alphabets, then spinning the circle to pick letters that form messages), and deja vu (sensing things happening in the present as though they have already happened).

Other gifts include:

- Hydromancy
- I Ching

- Libanomancy
- Precognition
- Oculomancy
- Scrying
- Tasseography
- Tarot reading
- Transfiguration
- Chiromancy
- Astrap projection
- Dream interpretation
- Megagnomy
- Energy healing
- Prophecy
- Past-life regression
- Other divination forms

Auric Layer

The auric field for this chakra comes from within the body and can be seen 2 ½ feet from your skin. The Ajna is in the brow, but that's just an external representation of the chakra. It's in the midbrain, behind your brows. It has several secondary chakras, which also work with the Sahasrara, Vishuddha, and Manipura.

A lot of systems have three major secondary chakras: soma, kamadhenu, and kameshvara. The soma lies in the sahsrara, above the third eye. It's a whitish or light blue lotus with either 12 or 16 petals, with a silver crescent. The moon creates the amrita nectar or oma, which flows forth from kamadhenu. Kamadhenu holds the cow goddess of the same name, who is also called the cow of plenty because she gives all desires. She came from an ocean of milk and dwelled in the heavens. This chakra connects the kameshvara to Ajna. The Kameshvara represents the male god of the same name, embracing Kameshvari, who happens to be a form of Kundalini. This is the area where she connects the Param Shiva in a union called tantra (expanded consciousness). This union is connected to yoga (or detachment) and bhoga (or enjoyment).

Within this chakra, you'll fin Kameshcara and Kamesvari surrounding a triangle known as A-KA-THA, formed by the vama, raudri, and jvestha nadis. When energy flows to Kameshvara, all your feelings, knowledge, and actions become goodness, beauty, and truth.

Exercise

For this exercise, you will use the mantra Thoh, pronounced like "toe." Make sure it's not high-pitched but not deep either. You'll know when you have the right tone. Before you begin, practice saying it in different tones. When you think you have the right tone, *you do.* Next:

1. Sit in a comfy, quiet place, with no distractions, keeping your back straight.

2. Inhale through your nose and hold the breath for as long as feels comfortable.

3. Part your lips slightly, keeping your jaw relaxed and both rows of teeth apart.

4. Put the tip of your tongue between both rows of teeth.

5. Apply light pressure to your tongue using your teeth, like you're about to say the word "the."

6. Now, slowly exhale through your mouth as you chant "T-h-h-o-o-h-h" with that breath. You need only one chant per exhale.

If you're doing this right, the air will flow past your teeth and tongue. You will notice a sensation or some pressure in your cheeks and jaw, and perhaps some vibration in your third eye. Chant this five times in a row, and do the exercise for three days straight, doing each session 24 hours after the last.

Chapter Nine: The Crown Chakra - Sahasrara

The seventh energy center is one with a thousand petals, symbolizing the limbic system's thousand nerve endings, the ends of the yoga nadis (one thousand of them), and your transcendence over the material world. Here, Shiva and Shakti are fully merged into one, forming brahmananda — brahman meaning "the Absolute," and ananda meaning "bliss." Therefore, this chakra is the doorway to pure consciousness, which will help you see that there's no better way to deal with your problems than to walk through them.

Sahasrara is an energy center intimately connected to the lower ones. Its subtle attributes are so unique that the ancients have placed it above the human body, though we now know that it is the top of your head. The Sahasrara is the completion of the last kosha, which is the anandamaya sheath serving as your causal body. It allows you to enjoy parama ananda, which is true bliss when you hit the superconscious state of a brahmavidvarishtha or guru. You drink deeply of the gods' nectar, and you play like the gods intended while loving your life.

Sahasrara translates to "thousand," referring to the "lotus of the thousand petals." It also means "dwelling place with no support" and "void." The petals are layered and have all the colors of the rainbow. This is the point of spirituality, and it lies in your cerebral cavity, connected to the cerebral plexus. It is gold, violet, or white. Like the Ajna, there's not a set age when it becomes active, but you could say it does so from ages 42 to 49.

Body Parts

The seventh chakra is connected to the pineal gland and the pituitary. The pineal gland is shaped like a pinecone. You can find it in the diencephalon portion of your brain, close to the pituitary gland, among other structures. It comprises neurons from your retina, routed there from the optical ganglia. It also has glial cells and pinealocytes, which are non-nerve cells that help to create melatonin and work with the nervous system in various ways. They help to make your pineal gland more sensitive to light.

Some glial cells are a part of your thought process and serve as the source of imagination. They use calcium to chemically relay messages, while other neurons rely on electrical signals for this purpose. They also work with other cells and organs to help you fight disease, heal injuries and neurons, and eliminate pathogens. They help make sure you have the right amount of neurotransmitters and ions and will serve as a gatekeeper, allowing some substances to pass through the blood-brain barrier to the brain and keep others out.

When you are exposed to artificial or extreme electromagnetic fields, the pineal is disturbed. Your immunity goes down, and more abnormal cells in the body lead to infertility, birth defects, cancer, and psychological issues like drug addiction. It can even lead to ADHD, depression, insomnia, and chronic pain when your pineal gland is under aroused by EMF. Overarousal also leads to issues like anxiety, anger, nightmares, aggressiveness, and impulsivity. Sunspots cause these conditions, an improper balance of dark and light rhythms, terrible nutrition, planet revolution, temperature swings, daily stress, and high altitudes.

You can fix the pineal by kindling, which involves training the neurons with positive EMF through meditation, constantly putting your brain in theta and alpha waves. These waves allow you to be creative and go to even deeper states of consciousness. Chants, mudras, shamanic drumming, and dancing can also help.

Body Parts

The sahsrara oversees the brain stem, pineal gland, cranial nerves, skull, cranial plexus, nervous system, cerebral cortex, cranium bones, brain, the top of your head, and the central nervous system. It also works with the brain's right eye and right hemisphere, while Ajna handles the left eye and left hemisphere.

Major Sense

The seventh chakra is beyond physical, so it has no sense or sense organ.

Action Organ

Even though it is beyond physical, you could call the pineal gland the organ in question.

Vital Breath

This energy center is beyond breath.

Related Illnesses

Skeletal disorders, muscular disorders, chronic exhaustion, depression, coordination issues, headaches and migraines, dizziness, amnesia, epilepsy, Alzheimer's, schizophrenia, Parkinson's psychosis, learning issues, insomnia, neurosis, sound and light sensitivity, and sensitivity to the environment are all related illnesses.

Psychology

The issues here concern your mental and emotional connection to virtues like consciousness, awareness, faith, hope, and truth. Every misconception leads to blocks that prop up karma rather than grace. It would be helpful to clear this stuff out by removing all conflict between you and your divine self.

Often, when you don't grasp spiritual issues or have no self-perception or self-love, illness abounds. You must learn to see that the Divine loves you and deems you worthy. This center also involves the matter of curses and possession. Some souls and energies belong to darkness and love to feast on those who seek to activate their seventh chakra. They seek to steal your light because they are jealous of what you have.

Archetypes

The positive archetype is the Guru, who unites analysis and intelligence to grasp the world. She is at one with the Divine and works with spiritual laws. The negative archetype is the Egotist, steeped in physicality, paying no mind to the physical.

Personality

The person with an evolved seventh chakra is very conscious, spiritual, and expresses universal truths. They love sacred philosophies, grasp good, evil, and bad, and are practical in helping others with their spiritual lives. They can perceive spirits and know how to be in a spiritual realm.

If this were you, you'd rather see the good in people, not the bad. Unfortunately, this can often lead you to unhealthy relationships, where you allow yourself to be lied to, abused, or demeaned as you wait for the good you genuinely believe is there. Remember to relate to people based on whom they show you they are and not who you think they can become.

Excesses and Deficiencies

Any deficiency here can lead to a lack of trust, joy, ethics, and purpose, and identity and meaning. You may become materialistic, apathetic, selfish, and unable to finish what you start. You may become afraid of spirituality or religion, make terrible decisions, and be cynical of all things spiritual. You might contend with learning issues, a fear of death, and a persistent feeling of being separate from others and alone. Extreme cases can lead to you neglecting what your body needs.

When there are excesses, you may become too intellectual, always living in your head, and thus, feeling superior to everyone around you. You can make a habit of hysterics, become manic-depressive, or even develop a fanatic addiction to a spiritual idea that doesn't serve you. In extreme cases, you may even disassociate from your body.

Balanced Sahasrara

When this center is balanced, you are no longer driven by the ego. You trust yourself more and are more selfless as your consciousness becomes superior while remaining tempered with empathy. You know how to see the big picture. You experience true satisfaction and inner peace and learn how to simply be in the moment. You also become able to both communicate and perceive, developing crown compassion. Your chakras balance out. In the first one, you experience groundedness; in the second, you get creative. In the third, you achieve worldly success. In the fourth chakra, your heart grows expansive. In the fifth, you become more expressive of your truth. In the sixth, you connect more with your inner knowing and intuition while achieving the highest state of consciousness in the Sahasrara itself.

Sahasrara Yantra

This yantra is complicated. It has a thousand petals and circular mon that sits in a golden pericarp. This moon is brilliant with light and is where immortality lies. It is cool and moist, just like nectar. In the moon is the triangle of light, pointing downwards, and in that is Shiva's circular home, which is also known as the Great Void or the prara bindu. This is the foundation of freedom, where Prama-Shiva dwells.

Parts of the Sahasrara

The gross element doesn't exist, as this center is unlimited. There is no subtle element, but the sound of the element is the Visarga, which is a breathing sound. It has the attributes of cosmic consciousness and nonduality. Its lotus petals are connected to a different nadi.

Cosmic Plane

This chakra is on the plane of truth or the satya loka.

Gods and Goddesses

Shakti is the sum of all her forms, with Shankhini as her final name. Once within Sahasrara and the supreme bindu, she is set free and now owns all her powers.

Shiva, or Adi Anadi, or the Supreme Divine Consciousness also rules here, representing the uncreated creator, pure consciousness, bliss, and liberation. Karma has no hold on him. When we reach Shiva, and the crown chakra becomes one with him, we too are free from all limitations. The ruling planet of this center is Uranus, an agent of change. There is no granthi with this one.

Psychic Abilities

When you are fully in charge of Sahasrara, you enter a state of supra consciousness and are wise; a jnani who doesn't think of the world as being apart from him, and at the same time doesn't assume that anything is his own. Instead, they no longer need to own things or control anything or anyone. Despite having access to all siddhis, the jnani doesn't feel the pull to use them and would rather reflect the Divine.

The gifts you gain are astral projection, exorcism, horoscopy, claircognizance, faith healing, recognition, prophecy, levitation, and empathic abilities.

Auric Layer

This layer is three feet away from the skin.

Secondary Chakras

The secondary chakras include:

- Mahanada
- Nirvana
- Guru
- Supreme Bindu

    The mahanada is where there's a higher vibration. It is connected to the thalamus gland, allowing psychic and mental abilities. It is plow-shaped, and gives boons peace, intelligence, and banishes fear. It allows you to be eloquent in speech.

    The nirvana is also called brahmarandhra. It is a multi-layered one, always connected to the crown chakra, and the end of the Sushumna at the cranium's top. It's also in the middle of the head, with one hundred petals of its own, serving as the seat of concentrated mind and your "I-ness." The guru or jnana chakra is what leads to knowledge, shows you the teacher within you, and keeps your mind pure. It is the light that drives off ignorance, which is darkness. Finally, the Supreme bindu is a point above your head.

Exercise

1. Lie on your back, shut your eyes, and progressively relax your muscles, beginning from the soles of your feet to the top of your head.

2. Set your left palm on your head gently and put the right hand over it.

3. Breathe in a relaxing, calming way.

4. As you breathe, allow your breaths to become deeper as you visualize yourself soaking up cosmic energy with each inhalation, and drive this energy to the Sahasrara with each exhalation.

5. Do this seven times as you visualize the life energy like a beam of light, violet in color. You could also imagine this flowing from your hands into your head and the rest of your body. You may see this light as clear and crystalline if you wish.

6. Hold your position for seven breaths (seven inhales and matching exhales).

7. When done, set your hands on the floor, by your body, and lie there enjoying how you feel in body, mind, and soul. Then open your eyes.

Chapter Ten: Meditation and Breathing Exercises

To keep your chakras balanced, it is vital that you keep up your physical and mental health. Therefore, meditation and breathing exercises are especially useful. With meditation, you can open your chakras and balance them out, leading to better health, mental clarity, and peace of mind.

Identifying Blocked Chakras

Your chakras could be closed, blocked, or imbalanced. When this happens, it doesn't receive the prana that flows through your body. To compensate, energy will flow to the healthier or more active chakras, but sadly, that's not enough. Some of them become "out of service," while others become overactive. These are situations you want to avoid, as you could have serious illnesses depending on the chakra in question and whether it is suffering from deficiencies or excesses. As such, you need to meditate so you can keep them all active and balanced.

The question is, how do you figure out which chakras are blocked or imbalanced? You can take chakra tests online, which will ask you questions about your personality, and then give you an arbitrary verdict about which of your chakras are hyperactive or blocked. Still, there is a much better way. Plus, now you have a much clearer understanding of chakras beyond just their colors, so you'll be able to discover for yourself. You have only to be on the lookout for any signs that there's something off with them.

Each chakra has a specific set of mental and physical symptoms that tell you whether there's not enough activity or too much of it. When you can tell what these symptoms are, you can pinpoint the ones that need work, so you can focus on restoring harmony and balance to the entire system.

Chakra Meditation

When the problematic energy center is identified, you have to do some work to fix it. One of the best methods there is to achieve that purpose is chakra meditation. This is not just any form of meditation. It's a special one designed to target all blocks in them with accuracy. When you can effectively use this recess, you will cleanse and clear out the energy centers. You will feel the balance in your body, mind, and day-to-day life experiences.

Controlling Your Chakras

Another way energy centers can be problematic is when they spin way too fast. This can harm you mentally and physically, so it is vital to learn to keep the energy flow in check. To do this, you need to meditate, and you can make meditation even more effective and laser-like by using mudras (finger positions) and mantras to help keep your awareness on the chakra in question.

Since the energy center is a part of a very intimate, intricate system, you can only do so much for each of these. So, it's more effective for you to meditate on all the centers to restore the whole system to a state of balance. The more you practice, you'll become better and better at pinpointing imbalances in specific chakras, so you can then focus the meditation on just the troublesome ones.

1. Find a quiet, comfy, peaceful place free of distractions. You should be able to stay here for 30 minutes at least, with no disturbance.

2. Sit on the floor in a comfortable position, folding your legs in the lotus. If this isn't comfortable, you may find a cushion to sit on.

3. Keep your spine as erect as you can while remaining relaxed.

4. Allow your hands to go limp on your knees.

5. Part your lips slightly, keeping your jaw nice and loose.

6. Begin to take deep and even breaths, inhaling through your nose and exhaling through your slightly parted lips.

7. As you breathe, begin to visualize or imagine each chakra, starting with the root, working your way up to the crown.

8. With each chakra, see the energy flowing into it and then through it. Imagine the colors for the chakra flowing in and out of it.

9. Be patient with each energy center and keep your awareness of it. Imagine that there's vibrant energy passing through the chakra with the light of its associated color.

10. As you breathe in, see the light go into the chakra and swirl around it, causing it to glow brighter if your imagination or visualization shows you it is dull.

11. As you exhale, see all blocks — like dark spots — leaving the chakra while it gets lighter and brighter. Be patient with this process. You'll need a few minutes for one. You may move on to the next one when the one you imagine looks and feels bright, balanced, and fine.

12. When you get to the Sahasrara, imagine that there's the pure life force flowing all through your body. Imagine that you're sitting at the bottom of an ocean of endless light, recharging you, refreshing you, and balancing out all chakras. Feel how wonderful that is.

If you're finding it hard to keep track of which center you're working with or maintaining your focus, you might find it helpful to look for guided meditations on the Internet because they can help you immensely with this problem. They usually have audio, images, and videos that can help you with pacing your meditation, so you don't rush through it, remaining focused on each center.

Working with Single Chakras

When you have made chakra meditation into a practice and a habit, you will start to feel a lot more sensitive to energy flow through the energy centers. You'll be better at connecting your physical and emotional states to the correct chakras. At this point, it will be helpful to start focusing on just individual chakras.

Whatever you do, you do not want to force this process. Allow yourself some time so you can gain proper experience. You will find you naturally shift your focus to the chakras that need the most work as you meditate when you do. You will also learn there are breathing exercises, mudras (gestures), poses, and mantras that can help you keep your attention on each chakra.

Muladhara Meditation

When you feel overwhelmed, uncertain, or unsettled, or you're working through a major challenge or changes in your life, then you should do this grounding meditation to balance your root chakra or activate it if it's not functional. This meditation is best done outside, but you can do it anywhere if going outside isn't an option for you. This won't affect the quality of your meditation, as energy is abundant and around us, unimpeded by the physical.

1. Sit on the ground. You may also sit on a chair. If you choose the chair, then you should keep your feet firmly on the ground. If you want, you may lay down on your back instead.

2. Shut your eyes. Become aware of the bottom of your spine.

3. Imagine that at the base of your spine, there's a sphere of light, ruby red. This light illuminates your pelvic floor.

4. See it radiate down your legs and into your feet. If you're lying down, see the light covering the whole area in contact with the ground.

5. Take deep breaths. With each one, imagine that energy comes up from the Earth and rises through your feet and legs (ida and Pingala) to your muladhara, rooting you firmly on the earth and in the moment.

6. As you inhale, draw the energy up through your feet and legs into the area right in front of your tailbone. Imagine this area glowing red, as the Muladhara should.

7. As you exhale, allow the energy to move back down into the earth.

You may play drumming or tribal music as you perform this meditation while chanting Lam to activate the element of Earth in your body.

Svadisthana Meditation

This exercise teaches you to develop faith in your emotional intelligence. It will help you process your emotions with ease, so you don't feel rigid or stuck. Take your time with this chakra so you can connect with your emotions better and process them in healthy, productive ways.

1. Sit down, so your hips are higher than your knees. This will allow your hips and lower back to relax.

2. Move your hips back and forth in a rocking motion so you can loosen up the area around your Svadisthana.

3. Begin to breathe in a deep, relaxed way.

4. Imagine that in between your navel and pubic bone, there is a breathtaking, beautiful Sun setting over the horizon of an ocean.

5. See the fiery light moving through your inner body while the orange glow reflects on the ocean's gentle waves.

6. Keep breathing deeply, and as you do, imagine these gentle waves are your breath. Your inhalation draws the waves onto the shore, and your exhales send them back to the sea. Your body may be still, but your breath continues to move, in and out, pausing with the stillness between waves.

7. As you keep this up, focusing on your breath and its connection with the water element, imagine that the movement of the wave is cleansing any emotional energy, through and through, leaving you completely clean and clear.

As you practice this meditation, it could help to listen to the sounds of the ocean, or even better, do this while you sit by an actual ocean or beach. As you meditate, you could chant Vam so the vibration of the element of water stays with you as you meditate and even after you're done.

Manipura Meditation

If you feel like you have no power, are insecure and unworthy, then your solar plexus needs a tune-up so you can remember your strength and power. This exercise will help you with discipline, courage, and confidence. It will help you channel your inner warrior in all your affairs.

1. Start by sitting in a comfy, quiet spot, spine erect yet relaxed.

2. Move your hands onto your belly, and then massage it using big, clockwise movements. This will help you rev up your digestive fire and keep your belly soft, as it gets tense whenever you feel unworthy. You want to make at least 7 of these circular massage movements, or 10, tops. Then set your hands down on your thighs.

3. Allow your breath to grow deeper and more relaxing.

4. As you exhale, tense your stomach muscles gently. As you inhale, allow your belly to get full and soft again. This is a great way to support the Ujjayo breath, a subtle one that allows your system to generate heat from within.

5. Imagine the fire element since it burns away all your feelings of inadequacy, fear, and being shackled by circumstances.

6. As you inhale, imagine that there's a bright flame that burns behind the navel, and as you exhale, blow out its smoke through your nose each time.

This is a great way to purify your stomach area and give support to your heart's desires so that you can act in self-confidence and with strength. You may want to practice this in front of a fire or with a lit candle. Besides seeing your fears burnt up by the flame within, you can also write all that bothers you on pieces of paper and then throw it into an actual fire. Chant Ram to set off the fire element.

Anahala Meditation

Do this meditation if you suffer from a broken heart or feel walled off or lonely. You will find you can connect to true, unconditional, objectless love when you do this. You will become more compassionate, generous, and resilient in the heart.

1. Begin by sitting tall, with your spine erect and your shoulder's back, yet relaxed. Sit in a proud posture, one that allows you to breathe deeply since the lungs are connected to the Anahata.

2. Start by imagining an emerald green light that fills your chest cavity.

3. Keep this light bright and burning by keeping your attention on it and breathing. Doing this will give even more strength to the shield, which keeps your heart safe from sorrow and challenges. Feed it by being aware of it and breathing so you can feel loved and safe.

4. When you've breathed this light into this space for several minutes, it's time to move your awareness to the middle of your chest. Imagine that there's a pink diamond in this position. This is your spiritual heart.

5. Imagine this pink diamond radiates a light that is soft and brings you peace. This light is who you are, beyond who you perceive yourself to be.

6. See and feel beauty, love, and goodness coming out of the diamond that is your heart, radiating throughout your body, washing over you. It allows you to share your beautiful light with one and all. It doesn't seek an object, person or circumstance to shine upon, as it is the very epitome of love, showing itself as you, through you.

> As you do this exercise, you could use rose essential oil. This oil is great for reducing stress, anxiety, and depression. You could also use the rose quartz crystal and/or actual roses as you meditate. Chant the Yam mantra, so your heart becomes open while remaining protected.

Vishuddha Meditation

> This is necessary to be able to express yourself in every way, on every level. It helps you with your artistic expression, creativity, and ability to live authentically.

1. Sit upright, in a comfy position.

2. Move your head and neck gently in a circle.

3. Keep your mouth closed but your jaw soft and unhinged so both rows of teeth are separate. Keep the lips and the skin around them relaxed.

4. Become aware of your throat and neck. Imagine a turquoise gem, brilliant and bright, right in the middle of this region. This gem is a symbol of your authenticity and truth and the magic you share with the universe. It is what holds your words, stories, art, and music. It is what connects your head and heart. Be aware of all of that.

5. Inhale as you imagine energy moving into the turquoise light at the middle of your throat.

6. Exhale, allowing this same energy to go out through your nose.

7. Imagine this light shines through your ears so that you're a better listener and can also hear your own inner voice. As you do this, you will improve your communication on all levels.

8. As you breathe, see yourself using your voice the right way, for the highest good.

> With this practice, you will find singing, chanting, and humming to be especially useful for the Vishuddha. You can play the music you resonate with or sing along to it. Chant Ham, as this opens your vocal cords and throat channel even more.

Ajna Meditation

This meditation will give you clarity of thought. It will help you to trust your intuition and expand your vision for what lies ahead of you. The more you meditate on your third eye, the easier you will find it to destroy all limiting patterns of thought and grow in imagination and wisdom.

1. Sit in a comfortable position and shut your eyes.

2. Turn your eyes, so they're focused on the spot between your brows, where the third eye lies. You want to make sure that the skin around both eyes is relaxed.

3. As you do this, imagine the deep royal blue or indigo of this chakra.

4. Move your awareness from your forehead to the middle of your brain. Contemplate the consciousness that allows you to see with your eyes and notice glimpses of it as it pops up between your ears as inner light.

5. As you do this, you will notice thoughts coming and going in your mind. Don't fight them. Let them pass on much like the clouds in the sky, and gently return your awareness to the middle of your brain. Do this as often as you drift in thought, lovingly. Never beat yourself up for losing focus; it happens.

6. To help you with this, you can put the tip of the tongue on your upper palate so it can also stimulate Ajna from beneath.

7. Throughout this exercise, breathe deep and steady.

You may try alternate nostril breathing to help you balance your mind and intuition. You can listen to classical music as you meditate, as this kind of music reduces stress and gives you a clear mind. You may also meditate in silence. If you wish to chant, use the Sham mantra.

Sahasrara Meditation

This meditation will keep you connected to your inner or higher self, or the Divine if you will. You will become closer to the reality of oneness. If you feel heavy, hopeless, and isolated, this is the practice to use because it will connect you to love, peace, and the meaning you seek.

1. Sit comfy, with your spine tall, pose proud, and regal.

2. Imagine that your head floats just like a lily on the water at the top of the spine.

3. Now, relax your jaw, neck, brow, and eyes.

4. Give the crown of your head a few taps so you can awaken and stimulate the Sahasrara.

5. In your mind's eye, see an invisible lotus that has a thousand petals at the top of your head. Lovingly and gently will it to open. This will allow you to have knowledge of self and truth.

6. See a purple column of light that comes out of the center of your head, shooting right into the sky. When you inhale, this energy column moves down, going into your body, filling it. As you exhale, it goes into the sky. This is the light of Divine consciousness.

7. When you sense completion, allow your awareness to move to the very middle of the invisible lotus. Give thanks to your higher self for graciously making itself known to you.

> As you practice this, you can amp up the effects by radiating gratitude. Gratitude moves you beyond the thoughts that bother your mind and right into the spiritual realm. Use amethyst to help you wake up your higher energy centers. If your mind and body still feel limited, you should try to get upside down by doing a headstand or hanging your head off the edge of a bed or sofa so the crown chakra receives energy.

Chapter Eleven: Positive Affirmations

To build your energy body and attain the spiritual heights you would like to achieve, you should never skip the elements of your practice that will lead to your enlightenment. One element is the use of positive affirmations.

Positive affirmations are amazing, whether you're using them to advance your career, develop better, healthier habits, or tap into your true identity. Used correctly, they can lead you to incredible success and growth. You have only to be consistent. Suppose you're dealing with troublesome emotions like anxiety, fear, worry, doubt, or a lack of self-love. There, you'll find that positive affirmation can help you put all of that to rest so you can channel your energy towards creating a world of good for you and others around you.

Again, positive affirmations are amazingly potent, and the same applies when it comes to chakra balancing, cleansing, and activating. At this point, you should know of the many benefits that are yours when your chakras work the way they should. So, it should be no news to you you should make a daily practice of keeping those energy centers healthy and functional.

Focusing on the Major Seven

There are other energy centers besides the main seven, and they all do their part to make sure the energy flows through your body as it should, but for now, we will stay focused on these. Typically, working with them will create a spillover effect, so your entire energy body reaps the rewards of your work.

It's not unusual for the chakras to move into an unbalanced state. You'll usually notice when this happens in your everyday life. The root chakra is in charge of your feelings of security and your survival instinct, for example. So, when there's an imbalance with this one, you might find you interact with everyone and everything around you from a place of distrust and cynicism. You might also suffer from anxiety, and physically, you may have to deal with gut issues.

If you've suffered a terrible situation or misfortune, then you'll be in a state of grief. This puts your Anahata out of balance, and so you must give it a boost. Here's another example: If you're in a situation where you need to speak up but find yourself unable or afraid to, then you will benefit from doing some energy work on your throat chakra — and positive affirmations.

Affirmations are crafted to allow you to bring balance to the problematic chakra so you can experience healing and allow energy to flow the way it should. Work with affirmations to restore yourself to a state that is in harmony and full of health. Another reason to adopt them is to help you to focus your attention and channel your awareness to where it matters. Of course, it also doesn't hurt you can practice them wherever and whenever to bring balance back to your entire self.

How to Work with Affirmations to Heal Your Chakras

You'd be hard-pressed to find a tool as potent and easy as positive affirmations, and there's a good reason for that. You see, your reality is the sum of the thoughts you entertain and the emotions you allow to be your permanent state of mind. So, using affirmations is a great tool for helping you shift from an unwanted state of mind and being to the preferred, balanced state.

Sometimes, we get into dark places and feel depressed. An effective way to help shift from a negative place in mind and emotion is to use positive affirmations to drum up positive energy, which will then lift you out of the dumps and put you in a place of power and clarity. Your chakras become free of all blockage, excesses, or deficiencies, and you get the corresponding effect in your daily life.

There are several reasons this process works so beautifully. For one thing, using this tool will allow you to connect with the natural healing energy that flows throughout the universe so you can easily use that energy to better your health, wealth, and life in general. This is the same energy that causes the Sun's rising and setting, holds all things on the planet in their place, and sustains all of life. You, too, can access this energy, and you can do that by using the power of positive words, which manifests your desires every time, in harmony with one and all.

Affirmations also help you to focus your mind, emotions, and entire being on whatever you intend to manifest. In this case, chakras and an entire energy body that works exactly as it's supposed to. It should be obvious that you can't afford to sleep on this. So, let's delve into how it works.

You will need to find somewhere quiet, where you can practice undisturbed. As always, please get rid of any distractions. Switch off your cell, ask the kids not to bother you for ten minutes at least, and wear loose clothing so that you're not distracted by discomfort.

Next, you need to sit comfortably and then place your focus or awareness on the spot where the chakra you want to work on lies. When you meditate, repeating your affirmation mindfully, you want to imagine the chakra's color and see that color moving into the spot where the energy center is as you repeat the affirmation.

Whatever you do, do not repeat this mindlessly like a broken record or something. You want to mean what you say each time, and you also want to feel the truth of those words welling up within you. Don't just mouth the words. Say them with conviction, and you will experience a powerful transformation.

Muladhara Affirmations

Remember, this chakra sits at the base of the spine and is red. It is the bedrock and foundation upon which all the others are built. It is the home of your survival instincts and needs and must be balanced so you can feel secure and stable. You'll see the evidence of that manifest in your life through material success and abundance. If not, you will find that you're easily angered, lazy, full of worry, and cling to people who make you feel safe. You might also have issues like lower back pain, menstrual cramps, constipation, and more. Use affirmations to fix all that.

As you make the following affirmations, you will notice you have more endurance, energy, strength, and will. You will feel very at one with nature, peaceful, and secure. You'll do more than survive; you'll thrive.

- I am safe.
- I am financially stable and secure.
- I am very taken care of.
- I am centered.
- I am always provided for.

Svadisthana Affirmations

This chakra is orange and halfway between your pelvis and navel. Since this chakra takes energy from Muladhara and uses it to drive creativity and pleasure, it's the one responsible for all your passion, energy, and joy in life. Out of balance, it causes you to lack self-control when it comes to sexual urges. You have no boundaries, suffer from sexual dysfunction, get obsessively attached, jealous, fearful, and all that yucky stuff.

Use these affirmations to help you be more positive about sex, your body, and your ability to create. They will help you to be more compassionate towards others, learning to love them, flaws and all. They'll keep you playful, optimistic, and vibrant.

- I am comfortable in my own skin.
- I am creative.

- I am comfortable with my sexuality.
- I am very aware of my feelings.
- I am joyful.
- I am open to pleasure and at peace with it.

Manipura Affirmations

This bright yellow energy center is in your belly, just beneath your heart, and concerns control, personal power, growth, and success. When it's not balanced, you suffer from fear and anxiety, and this can further deteriorate into resentment and unhealthy competition. Use these affirmations to tap into and get better at using your innate talents, and learn to be assertive and confident with boundaries founded on compassion. This way, you'll know who you are and come to trust yourself more and more.

- I honor myself.
- I am powerful.
- I have ease and flow in all I do.
- I am grateful.
- I am strong.
- I am the power that sustains and creates worlds.

Anahata Affirmations

This vibrant green chakra is in your chest, between the breasts, and over the heart. This chakra allows you to experience and give compassion, unconditional love, and generally feel well. It connects the lower centers with the higher ones. When you feel isolated and lonely, or you are stuck in relationships that are the very definition of dysfunction, dealing with the fear of rejection, jealousy, criticism, and being clingy and codependent, this is the chakra to balance. If you have problems with your upper back, heart, and lungs, then these affirmations can help you. As you affirm the following, you will become more empathetic, accepting, and welcoming of others the way they are. You will grow in love, wisdom, and emotional intelligence.

- I love myself.
- I accept myself.
- I receive love freely.

- I give love freely.
- I am open to love fully.
- I have a heart overflowing with love.

Vishuddha Affirmations

This blue chakra in your throat determines your ability to express yourself, communicate with others, and be honest. If out of balance, you're afraid to speak up when you should, and you deal with confusion and embarrassment from saying things you shouldn't. You might find you gossip often and feel a need to lie. An out of balance Vishuddha can lead to issues with your gums and teeth, laryngitis, stiffness in your neck, and other physical discomforts.

Use these affirmations to develop clear, confident, and compassionate self-expression, a strong voice, the ability to listen excellently, and artistic self-expression.

- I trust others.
- I trust myself.
- I speak my truth in freedom and love.
- I enjoy expressing myself with my voice.
- I am always honest about who I am.
- I am safe to voice my needs.

Ajna Affirmations

The indigo Ajna is in the middle of your brows and concerns clarity, intuition, and your connection to the spiritual realms. Out of balance, you have issues prioritizing, have no perspective, and could never be described as a person of imagination. You find it hard to focus and to hold on to information. Use these affirmations so you can connect with spiritual truth and wisdom in your everyday life. You will feel a sense of peace beyond all comprehension and a connection with the Source.

- I am connected to Source/the Divine.
- I am clear in thought every time.
- I trust my intuition always.
- I intimately know my true voice.
- I am full of peaceful thoughts.

Sahasrara Affirmation

This violet energy center is at the top of your head, and why you can attain enlightenment and become spiritually awake and aware. Out of balance, you will feel overwhelmed and an odd detachment from real life. If you haven't activated the lower chakras and you force energy to Sahasrara, you may have issues like addictions and spiritual crises. Use these affirmations to feel more connected with the world around you and set yourself free from spiritual shackles. You'll also become at one with Source and have access to immeasurable wisdom.

- I am at peace.
- All things are connected.
- I am divinity in the flesh.
- I am connected to the All.
- All is well.

Chapter Twelve: Developing Your Psychic Abilities

There is a difference between developing spiritually, and developing your psychic abilities, although one can lead to the other when done right. When you're psychic, you can read people and places just by energy. As for spiritual development, it involves growing on all levels where you exist, in all aspects of life, developing your thoughts, understanding the reason you are alive, and why your relationships with yourself and others matter.

In other words, you can be psychic and still spiritually underdeveloped. The trouble with this is that it can cause you to become very centered on your ego. However, developing yourself spiritually will give you richer, more meaningful connections with the world around you, so you always come from a place of empathy, from the heart. This is the best route to take, considering your psychic abilities will develop at the same time.

So, while having psychic powers is cool and all, you want to approach this with the sincere desire to develop your spirit while developing your psychic abilities. Make this simultaneous, and there will be harmony in your life, as you bring together every part of you into one balanced whole.

Chakras and Psychic Abilities

To develop your abilities, consider what you're naturally good at, intuitively speaking. This means becoming more aware of your chakras. They allow your abilities to come through and be the path you take to develop spiritually.

The seven energy centers have their own unique gifts.

- Muladhara gives you information from other dimensions.
- Svadisthana improves your intuition.
- Manipura gives you those "gut feelings."
- Anahata balances energies from the spiritual and physical realms.
- Vishuddha allows you to communicate, and of all chakras, it has the most psychic senses.
- Ajna gives you psychic visions and psychic intuition.
- Sahasrara is what ties you to your higher self and all things spiritual.

With these energy centers, we often give and get information, whether we're conscious of it or not. They are especially useful for picking up on subtle, psychic messages. You'd have a hard time manifesting these abilities without having these chakras active and open first. Many people have chakras that are naturally active, which means they naturally have psychic abilities that correlate to those chakras. Though, if you weren't "born this way," you must open your chakras first. Think of them like a door or a psychic portal that allows you access to all sorts of dimensions and information energetically. As you open them, you will become more and more aware of your gifts.

Meditation

Meditation is key for opening your centers up because it's a great way to keep your awareness centered where it should be. By channeling your focus on each chakra for just five to ten minutes daily, you will notice your intuition and awareness growing to greater levels. Here's how to meditate so that you can improve energy flow and increase your psychic abilities.

1. Sit somewhere quiet and get in an upright position. You may lay flat on your back if you prefer.

2. Inhale, and as you do, see energy as white light in your mind's eye, coming up and moving through your body, flowing directly into the blocked chakra.

3. Exhale, leaving that energy locked in there. Notice the chakra glowing brighter, looking more vibrant and alive than before (in your imagination).

4. Inhale again, drawing in more energy, and then exhale, locking it in, seeing a brighter glow.

5. Continue this for some minutes.

6. You can now put your palm on the chakra, directing energy to and through it for 15 minutes. You might notice some cool, warm, burning, or tingling sensations in there, during or after meditation. This is simply your chakra receiving energy.

You can do this with all chakras. The key is to be consistent. A fair warning: You might notice no substantial change for weeks or even months but stay consistent and patient. In time, you may notice you are much more psychically aware and that you're developing certain abilities.

The Third Eye and Psychic Development

The third eye is important when it comes to developing psychic powers because it regulates your subtle body's energy flow. It gives the wisdom and understanding needed to comprehend life beyond the physical. It allows you to get past the idea of duality and become more aware of the truth of who you are, a spirit having an adventure as a human. You are more than your flesh.

For some people, the level of spiritual awareness they get through developing this center can be incredibly overwhelming, especially when they have done no work on the lower five centers. So, again, never try to run before you can stand. Work with your chakras, beginning from the root and then moving on up. Don't rush this process.

When you have worked through everyone and approach the third eye, it opens as it should with no terrible side effects. You will notice you have an inner knowing of sorts. You will also sense the fullness of your being, "I Am." You will find that your emotions, beliefs, fears, and judgments are simply experiences and not the definition of who you are.

Opening Ajna

When your third eye is open, you see yourself laid bare before you. There's no room for self-deceit. You can see your insecurities, false assumptions, and judgments. You can see when playing the victim. You'll also notice the many different hats you have when it comes to interacting with people. You can see when you connect with others based on their thoughts and assumptions about your person, and you can step beyond all that and the illusions by which most define their everyday lives. Know you will become aware of a spiritual reality before you do this, which means your sense of identity will change. Accept this, and you will be fine.

Exercise 1

1. Sit somewhere quiet, where you won't be bothered. You'll need a pen and a notepad.

2. Think about who you are right now.

3. Write down as many sentences as you can, in a list form, beginning with the words "I am." You could write, "I am beautiful, I am a wife, I am a writer, I am lonely, and so on."

4. Next, think about how you were ten years before now.

5. Create another list based on who you were back then.

6. Pick two more periods from these times, and then repeat the process.

7. Now, look through all lists, and notice the differences. Notice how your self-perception shifted and changed over time.

Exercise 2

With this exercise, you're going to act. Don't worry; you don't need to win an Oscar. When you act, you can access so many emotions, and those emotions usually affect the way you behave and how you perceive yourself. You're going to generate emotions using your memory.

1. Recall a funny experience. Make yourself laugh at it. Force the laughter, if you must, until it's natural.

2. Recall a sad experience. Make yourself cry – and feel it.

3. Recall an infuriating experience. Scream angrily into a pillow, saying whatever you want.

The key to this exercise is to exaggerate the feelings but don't remain in these feelings for long. What you will learn from this is that emotions do not define you. You are not your emotions.

Exercise 3

This exercise involves keeping a dream journal. When you dream, your third eye is active. The more you journal your dreams, the easier you will recall future ones, and the more detailed they become. You will also become more connected to your unconscious, which is the home of all your blind spots. Have a dream journal app on your phone to make things easier for you.

1. When you wake up from bed, don't move. Just lie there.

2. Remember the last thing that happened in your dream.

3. Work your way backward.

4. Once you've got most of the dream, open your dream journal.

5. Write down the key images you saw that would remind you of each part of the dream so you don't lose that memory.

6. Now, write out the dream in detail, referring to the keywords to make sure you're not leaving anything out.

7. As you go to bed each night, run through your day in reverse until you hit the point when you woke up in the morning because doing this will help you with dream recall.

8. As you fall asleep, gently affirm to yourself with conviction, "My dreams are crystal clear. I remember them all."

The Underrated Vishuddha

The third eye chakra is powerful, but the throat chakra is the main psychic center, housing three of your psychic senses. Clairvoyance allows you to see without *physical* eyes. You get images of places, people, and events using your third eye, and you can also see past the illusion of the physical realm or maya. When you have clairvoyance, you can enter a room and perceive energetic images and imprints of what's been going on before you got there. This ability sits in the brow chakra.

Clairsentience is clear feeling and sensing, and this ability is in the Svadisthana. When you have this ability, you can feel emotions and things like cold and heat even though it isn't cold or hot. You are an empath. This is usually the very first of the psychic senses that most people develop and comes before the third eye's abilities.

Now the throat chakra is what holds three psychic abilities, including clairgustance, clairscent, and clairaudience. With clairaudience, you hear things without needing your actual ears. This easily lends itself to telepathy. You can get information from the spirit or hear messages about past events or experiences that have been energetically imprinted in a place. Clairscent allows you to smell things that aren't there. If you have ever smelt a perfume of a loved one who isn't around, and they didn't just spray it recently, then you've experienced this. If they've passed on, it means they're right there with you. Clairgustance allows you to taste without needing to use your tongue. It might seem like quite an odd ability, but it's pretty useful. For instance, getting a terrible, metallic taste in your mouth if you're interacting with someone could tell you about the state of his or her health.

Since Vishuddha has more psychic senses than other chakras, you need to keep this chakra balanced to develop your psychic power. If you intend to work as a healer, pay attention to this chakra to work with it well. As a healer, you must pass on valuable information and use your skills to the best of your abilities during your sessions. You cannot give your best if your throat chakras and others aren't in alignment. Only when balanced, healthy, and aligned can your psychic abilities work as they should. When you give attention to the throat chakra, nurturing it, you must be a psychic powerhouse, functioning at an energetic rate (high and efficient), being a blessing to those around you when you share your gifts with them.

Conclusion

We have finally come to the end of this book, and what a trip it has been! You know all you need to about chakras. Now, you could always go out and seek more information — and in fact, you should. However, more knowledge will not spur you on to actual spiritual and psychic growth. The key is to begin an actual practice if you haven't already.

This is as good a time as any to let you know that you shouldn't beat up on yourself for not being able to "visualize." Unfortunately, many people hear that word and think that they're supposed to see an actual image pop up in their view, but that's not the case.

Visualizing simply involves imagining. That's it. If you have issues with imagining images, you can imagine sensations instead and improvise with the exercises. Simply placing awareness on any energy center is more than enough to awaken and stimulate it. The exercises given here help you keep your focus on these centers longer, so you do not drift off in the middle of an exercise.

A Word of Caution: Do not seek to attain psychic powers just for their sake. It's not impossible, but there are consequences that you should be aware of. This is a surefire path to becoming imprisoned in illusions about reality and the self. So, the question is, how do you go about this without making it about wanting to have "supercool powers?" It's simple—root everything you do and say in love.

When you come from a place of love, it makes it hard for you to become arrogant or egocentric with your abilities. For instance, certain people with the ability to speak something and then have it come to pass. This is the gift of prophecy — not based on impressions they get energetically, but their ability to affect physical life. Now, imagine being selfish person with this ability and is wrongfully crossed by someone. If you come from love, you wouldn't prophesy their death or illness or something. You wouldn't use your powers that way. Yet, if you did that, then you are demonstrating to the spirit you aren't ready to develop and grow beyond where you are — and the thing is, there is always more! But you won't get that because you're irresponsible with the little you do have.

To summarize:

1. Continue with your practice.
2. Become like a child, curious about the world you see and worlds that may be but aren't immediately obvious.
3. Always use it every time something stands out to you in an odd way, or you get a weird thought or feeling.
4. Always acknowledge every little manifestation of your abilities because the more you do, the more they will grow.

References

Apte, Vaman Shivram (1965). The Practical Sanskrit Dictionary (fourth revised & enlarged ed.). Delhi: Motilal Banarsidass Publishers. ISBN 81-208-0567-4.

Bucknell, Roderick; Stuart-Fox, Martin (1986). The Twilight Language: Explorations in Buddhist Meditation and Symbolism. London: Curzon Press. ISBN 0-312-82540-4.

Flood, Gavin (1996). An Introduction to Hinduism. Cambridge: Cambridge University Press. ISBN 0-521-43878-0.

Chia, Mantak; Chia, Maneewan (1993). Awaken Healing Light of the Tao. Healing Tao Books.

Dale, Cyndi (2009). The Subtle Body: An Encyclopedia of Your Energetic Anatomy. Boulder, Colorado: Sounds True. ISBN 978-1-59179-671-8.

Monier-Williams, Monier. A Sanskrit-English Dictionary. Delhi: Motilal Banarsidass Publishers.

Prabhananda, S. (2000). Studies on the Tantras (Second reprint ed.). Calcutta: The Ramakrishna Mission Institute of Culture. ISBN 81-85843-36-8.

Rinpoche, Tenzin Wangyal (2002). Healing with Form, Energy, and Light. Ithaca, New York: Snow Lion Publications. ISBN 1-55939-176-6.

Saraswati, Swami Sivananda (1953–2001). Kundalini Yoga. Tehri-Garhwal, India: Divine Life Society. Foldout chart. ISBN 81-7052-052-5.

Woodroffe, John (1919–1964). The Serpent Power. Madras, India: Ganesh & Co. ISBN 0-486-23058-9.

Saraswati, Swami Sivananda (1953–2001). Kundalini Yoga. Tehri-Garhwal, India: Divine Life Society. ISBN 81-7052-052-5.

Goswami, Shyam Sundar. Layayoga: The Definitive Guide to the Chakras and Kundalini, Routledge & Kegan Paul, 1980.

Sharp, Michael (2005). Dossier of the Ascension: A Practical Guide to Chakra Activation and Kundalini Awakening (1st ed.). Avatar Publications. ISBN 0-9735379-3-0. Archived from the original on 21 December 2012.

Khalsa, Guru Dharam Singh; O'Keeffe, Darryl. The Kundalini Yoga Experience Simon & Schuster, 2002.

Judith, Anodea (1996). Eastern Body Western Mind: Psychology and the Chakra System As A Path to the Self. Berkeley, California, USA: Celestial Arts Publishing. ISBN 0-89087-815-3

www.ingramcontent.com/pod-product-compliance
Lightning Source LLC
Chambersburg PA
CBHW081622100526
44590CB00021B/3561